High Performing Investment Teams

High Performing Investment Teams

How to Achieve Best Practices of Top Firms

Jim Ware and Jim Dethmer

With Jamie Ziegler and Fran Skinner

WILEY

John Wiley & Sons, Inc.

Published by John Wiley & Sons, Inc., Hoboken, New Jersey.
Published simultaneously in Canada.

For general information on our other products and services or for technical support, please contact our Customer Care Department within the United States at (800) 762-2974, outside the United States at (317) 572-3993 or fax (317) 572-4002.

Wiley also publishes its books in a variety of electronic formats. Some content that appears in print may not be available in electronic books. For more information about Wiley products, visit our web site at www.wiley.com.

Library of Congress Cataloging-in-Publication Data

Ware, Jim, 1954-
  High performing investment teams : how to achieve best practices of top firms / by Jim Ware and Jim Dethmer With Jamie Ziegler and Fran Skinner ; foreword by Michael J. Mauboussin ; afterword by Kate Ludeman and Eddie Erlandson.
    p. cm.
  Includes bibliographical references.
  ISBN-13 978-0-471-77078-7 (cloth)
  ISBN-10 0-471-77078-7 (cloth)
  1. Investment advisors.   2. Teams in the workplace.   3. Leadership.   I. Dethmer, Jim.
II. Title.
  HG4621.W36 2006
  658.15'2—dc22
                                                                    2005029718

Printed in the United States of America.

10 9 8 7 6 5 4 3 2 1

Contents

Foreword

Michael J. Mauboussin

Shortly after his retirement, Jack Welch, the legendary CEO of General Electric, spoke to a group of 5,000 human resources (HR) executives and delivered a message he was sure they would appreciate: *The head of HR should be the second most important person in any organization.* Anticipating some audience adulation, he was surprised when a strange hush filled the room. Prodding, he asked how many of the participants worked for firms where the CEO treated the head of HR and the CFO with equal respect. Only 50 hands went up.

Welch was astounded. Ninety-nine percent of these companies emphasized finance over people! "If you managed a baseball team," he asked, "would you listen more closely to the team accountant or the director of player personnel?" Put this way, the lack of focus on people and their behavior seems absurd, yet this is how most executives manage their companies today.

If the only lesson you learn from *High Performing Investment Teams* is that people are crucial to long-term success, you will be ahead of the game and your competition. Still, this book offers much more than that seemingly simple lesson. The Focus team deftly guides you through both the theory and the practice of what makes investment firms thrive, and provides you with concrete cases and tools to improve individual and team behavior.

Psychologists find that people tend to attribute actions more to an individual's character than to the social context, or the situation, in which the individual operates. Studies show, though, that social context has an extremely powerful influence on behavior. Researchers have consistently noted that when good people discover themselves in bad situations, their behavior changes for the worse. Thus, even if the need is not obvious or intuitive, creating a favorable social context is vital to any investment organization that wants to sustain above-average performance.

Even as star money managers (including my esteemed colleague Bill Miller) adorn investment magazine covers, academic research shows that a substantial majority of fund results are attributable to the investment firm, not a particular individual. No doubt there are super-talented money managers out there, but performance starts and stops with them unless they create an enduring, high-performing organization.

Mastering the seven behaviors of high-performing teams is a challenge for any business. Investment professionals may have an even more difficult time adopting these behaviors than people in most industries, aside from the personality issues the Focus team correctly considers. Specifically, investment managers face three hurdles to organizational development. The best firms work hard to clear all three.

The first challenge is the probabilistic nature of markets. Like a coin toss, you never know for sure what's going to happen next. As a result, the link between process (how an organization makes a decision) and outcome (the result of that decision) is weak in the short to medium term. This is crucial because an investment firm may employ a poor process and still enjoy favorable short- to medium-term outcomes by sheer chance. These results invariably lead executives to overlook process and leave well enough alone. Only after the performance wheels come off (which is inevitable) will a firm reassess its process and people. By then, it's often too late.

Saying it somewhat differently, the feedback loop is not very tight in financial markets. As a result, investment results do not always provide management with an accurate picture of investment team performance. This means that organizational problems can fester undetected for longer than they should, and the efforts and methods of high-performing teams may not appear fruitful for uncomfortably long stretches of time.

This leads to the second challenge: Markets evolve. Investors frequently look to the past when trying to divine the future, hoping that past patterns will repeat themselves. The hard truth is that the past applies only when the conditions (for example, interest rates, inflation, tax policy) have not changed much. When lots of change occurs, all bets are off.

Market evolution argues strongly for the significance of continuous learning, but it also exacts a toll. Investors often exhaust their energy sorting through a torrent of external information instead of allocating attention inside the investment organization to cultivate the behaviors that help detect and cope with change.

The final, and perhaps the greatest, hurdle is the substantial agency costs in the investment industry today. Within most firms, there is a tension between the investment *profession*—delivering superior results to investors over time—and the investment *business*—maximizing assets and fees. Increasingly, the incentives of agents (the investment managers) to maximize their own welfare take precedence over maximizing wealth for the principals (investors). When an investment firm focuses [more] on marketing than on markets, the day-to-day activities of front-[line invest]ment professionals do not align with their ostensible goal. This [divergence] undermines the behaviors associated with high-[quality investing.] Incentives are a powerful force in the investment [business, and aligning inc]entives with behaviors is a crucial task.

[In my years in the in]vestment business, I have had the opportunity [to visit investme]nt firms around the world. In those [visits, I have liste]ned to their frustrations, and [I have seen an indust]ry full of talented, dedicat-[ed people who, eith]er wittingly or unwit-[tingly, confront forces tha]t constrain their

room [   ] here is
take you to [   ] will
comprehensive [   ]
applying these princi[ples]

Preface

This book is the logical sequel to our first book, *Investment Leadership*, which discusses the steps in creating a vision and building a winning investment culture. That book identifies the specific elements of leadership that contribute to an investment firm's sustainable success, and covers the importance of clearly defining the vision and values. (The first chapter of the present book reviews the major concepts of *Investment Leadership*.)

High Performing Investment Teams investigates the specific behaviors that are implied by values such as "accountability" or "lifelong learning" or "teamwork." What does it mean to be accountable? Or to be a great team player? "It turns out your high-school coach was right: Teamwork matters," wrote Scott Thurm in *The Wall Street Journal*.[1] "Research from a variety of settings, from hospital operating rooms to Wall Street, suggests that the way people work together is important for an endeavor's success—even in fields thought of as dominated by individual 'stars.' The studies may offer lessons for executives on boosting productivity and innovation."

We present an overview of all this material in the introduction, and then dedicate the chapters to in-depth investigation of these seven specific behaviors. Along with the discussion and tools for making your own progress, we provide research support and reports of hands-on experience to support all our contentions and conclusions.

Before we move into the behaviors themselves, a word on the writing of this book. We chose to make this a collaborative effort, which is no surprise given our bias and business. Although Jim Dethmer, Jack Skeen, and Jim Ware wrote the chapters, each of our team members contributed significantly to the ideas, examples, and editing of this book. Thus, the author credit at the beginning of each chapter is primarily for convenient reference when we use first-person examples in our writing (for example, "I," "me," "my early experience," or "my wife and our kids").

Acknowledgments

We view ourselves as chemists who bring together different elements to create new applications. *Investment Leadership* merged the work of Jim Collins and Jerry Porras in *Built to Last* (1994) and *Good to Great* (2001) and Richard Barrett's *Liberating the Corporate Soul* (1998) with the world of investments to explain how investment leaders can most effectively leverage their cultures for long-term success. In *High Performing Investment Teams*, we bring the work of Gay and Katie Hendricks and Kate Ludeman and Eddie Erlandson to the world of asset management. The behaviors described in this book are taken directly from the work of the Hendricks, Ludeman, and Erlandson. These behaviors have changed our lives—both the way we work and the way we live. Quite frankly, we teach these behaviors to investment professionals because they have made such a difference to us and we see them making a huge difference to people who run money for a living.

So, Gay and Katie and Kate and Eddie: thank you! We appreciate you for modeling and mentoring a radical way of being in the world. Here's to "smuggling donkeys!"

Our sincere appreciation also goes to Jeff Diermeier, Rebecca Fender, Julie Hammond, and our many friends at the CFA Institute for their ongoing invitations to present our new material at their conferences, at their workshops, on their webcasts, in their management newsletter, and at their member societies around the world.

We thank David Tittsworth at the Investment Adviser Association for inviting us to present at his Board of Governors events and for hosting our teambuilding workshops. Similarly, we thank Fred Bleakley for his invitation to join the Institutional Investors' Senior Delegates Roundtable.

A long list of clients and friends graciously shared with us many stories about their successes—as well as their challenges—with teamwork at their organizations. We deeply appreciate them for their candor and insights, and for their permission to include or reflect these stories throughout this book. In addition, many of them reviewed this manuscript and gave us valuable feedback. Our thanks to them all:

> Marie Arlt, Ted Aronson, Jim Bary, Peter Bernstein, Gary Brinson, Deb Brown, Jeff Brown, Erick Busay, Glenn Carlson, Bob Chapelle, Gary Clemons, Harin Da Silva, Nate Dalton, Michael Daubs, Beth Ann Day, Stephen Dunn, Sheldon Dyck, Richard Ennis, Don Ferris, Gordon Fines, David Fisher, Roger Fox, Mike Gasior, Larry Gibson, Dana Hall, Brit Harris, Bud Haslett Jr., Mellody Hobson, Marilyn Holt-Smith, Steve Holwerda, Jennifer Hom, Jon Hunt, Steve Joyce, Steve Kneeley, Bill Koehler, Isadora Lagos, Richard Lannamann, Bill Lyons, Michael Mauboussin, Marc Mayer, Chris McConnell, Will McLean, Donna Merchant, Jennifer Murphy, Bill Nutt, Raymond Orr, Lisa Parisi, Art Patten, Barry Paul, Wendell Perkins, Scott Powers, Al Prentice, Bill Quinn, Bill Raver, Sam Reda, Kim Redding, John Rogers, Alison Rogers-McCoy, Richard Rooney, Jim Rudd, Michael Sapir, Derek Sasveld, Dr. Andreas Sauer, Michelle Seitz, Craig Senyk, Kim Shannon, Brian Singer, Alvin Specter, Richard Steiny, Andy Stephens, Mike Steppe, Peggi Sturm, Nick Tannura, David Tittsworth, Terry Toth, Ted Truscott, Liz Uihlein, Tom Weary, Beth Whalen, Thurman White, Michael Yoshikami, John Zerr, and Jim Zils.

We are fortunate to have the wonderful support of our administrative partner, Beth Tuttle, particularly as we pulled this book together, experimenting with different forms of composition and style. With the precision of a professional lab technician, Beth skillfully orchestrated all the logistics in the compilation of the manuscript, without missing a beat in her day-to-day administrative responsibilities.

Of course, our heartfelt gratitude goes to our families, particularly our spouses—Jane, Debbie, Linda, Stuart, and Chuck—who lent their support and encouragement during every phase of this project.

About the Authors

Jim Ware, CFA, is the founder of the Focus Consulting Group, a specialized firm dedicated to helping investment leaders understand, articulate, and shape their firm's investment culture so it can be leveraged for investment success. Jim is also a highly acclaimed industry author and international speaker on the subjects of investment leadership, culture, and building of high-performing investment teams. He is the lead author of *Investment Leadership: Building a Winning Culture for Long-Term Success* (Hoboken, N.J.: John Wiley & Sons, 2004). Jim's quarterly newsletter, "Managing the Firm," is featured on the CFA Institute web site. Jim has 20 years' experience as a director of buy-side investment operations, a research analyst, and a portfolio manager. He holds an MBA from the University of Chicago and a BA in philosophy from Williams College.

Jim Dethmer, a principal with the Focus Consulting Group, is a world-class coach, speaker, and team-builder. He has lectured before more than 250,000 people worldwide and has worked with teams and executives from leading investment organizations, strengthening their effectiveness through customized coaching and consulting interventions. His keen insights and straightforward delivery of powerful and practical principles enable individuals, teams, and organizations to achieve breakthrough results in personal growth and profitability. Additionally, Jim has been featured on webcasts for the CFA Institute, covering the topics of world-class decision making and the essential behaviors of high-performing investment teams. Jim holds a BS in business management from Texas Christian University.

Jamie Ziegler is a principal with the Focus Consulting Group, responsible for client relations and marketing. Jamie's expertise in branding and marketing communications is drawn from more than 20 years of investment experience, working with investment firms of all sizes. Jamie previously served as senior vice president of global marketing for Northern Trust Global Investments and as director of marketing/product management for Stein Roe & Farnham, Inc. Jamie began her career as a mutual fund analyst and has co-authored books and other publications on mutual fund investing. She holds a BA in English from the University of Notre Dame and an MBA in finance from DePaul University.

Fran Skinner, CFA, CPA, has 19 years of experience in the financial services industry with Mellon Bank, Allstate Investments, and the Focus Consulting Group. In addition to managing the back- and middle-office functions for various investment asset types, Fran has worked extensively with senior management on strategic planning, cash management, competitive compensation, succession planning, and design and monitoring of investment performance goals. Drawing on her creativity and extensive experience in the investment industry, she also specializes in designing and delivering customized training for investment firms, such as hiring for cultural fit and other special topics, and leading special projects for senior investment management. Fran has an MBA in Marketing and Finance from the University of Illinois–Chicago.

Jack Skeen, PhD, author of Chapter 8, has been studying and working in the area of human potential and coaching for the past 35 years. He has served as mentor and coach for many CEOs and senior executives of Fortune 500 companies. He is exceptionally talented at identifying obstacles that create a "ceiling effect" to success for individuals, relationships, and teams. Before entering the world of coaching, Jack founded a private psychotherapy practice, where he worked for 10 years. He holds advanced degrees in theology from Westminster Theological Seminary and a PhD in psychology from Biola University.

Introduction
The Elements of Greatness

Jim Ware

Greatness, it turns out, is largely a matter of conscious choice.
—Jim Collins

Seated next to the CEO of a large real estate investment company, I listened to him describe the history of his firm as our flight took off from the Jacksonville airport. He talked about the difficult years in the early 1990s and the success his firm had achieved by the turn of the century. This CEO had heard me present at the conference we had both attended and knew that my firm specializes in leadership, culture, and team-building in the investment world. He used the opportunity on the plane to ask my advice about an incident at a recent offsite meeting he had held with his senior staff. He described it this way: "There were 10 of us at the table, and we were discussing strategies for the following year. After about an hour, one partner looks across the table at another team member and announces to the group, 'You know, I just don't like you.'" At this point, the CEO put his cup on the tray table, looked at me, and said, "So, Mr. Culture Expert, what do you do with that situation?"

This conversation is a perfect place to start, because this book is about the rules of engagement for high-performing investment teams. The problem with my seatmate's real estate team was that its members had never consciously discussed their rules of engagement. There was no context in which to place the comment: "I don't like you." (The CEO in question dealt with it by taking the offender to the woodshed and summarily scolding him.)

On the best teams, many of which are ones we've had the privilege of working with, there are clear rules of engagement and ways to handle conflicts, disagreements, trust issues, and broken agreements. This book is about the behaviors of high-performing teams. The word *behaviors* is carefully selected, because it means actions over which we have choice. The behaviors described in this book can be chosen and performed by anyone. This is different from personal attributes over which people have little or no control, such as intelligence or left-handedness. In fact, control is an important concept in this book. The very best-performing teams and individuals have learned to focus almost exclusively on things they have control over and not to concern themselves with the things that are out of their control.

Jim Collins, author of *Built to Last* and *Good to Great*,[1] made this same point when talking about success: "Do you believe that your ultimate outcomes in life are externally determined—'I came from a certain family, I got the right job'? Or do you believe that how your life turns out is ultimately up to you, that despite all the things that happen, you are ultimately responsible for your outcomes?"[2] Collins then cited the example of Southwest Airlines, which has been a huge success story in a difficult industry. The best-performing teams, like the Southwest Airlines employees, share a belief that they are responsible for what they create as a team, and that they can choose rules of engagement (such as behaviors) that will contribute to their highest effectiveness and best results.

Because we conduct surveys on investment teams from around the world, we have insights into trends in leadership and culture. Interestingly, as of the publication date of this book, the number-one value that investment firms aspire to have is "collaboration/teamwork." It is one of the top 10 values chosen by every single investment firm we have surveyed. In an industry renowned for stars and individual contribution, we find this a remarkable statistic. Both international and U.S.-based investment firms are taking seriously the notion that superior investment decisions and results are the product of a team's work, not that of one gifted individual. Because we have had the good fortune to work with some of the industry's geniuses, such as John Rogers, Charles Brandes, and many others, we can say with certainty that they, too, believe in the power of a collaborative culture. Perhaps the most unique approach to teamwork is offered by a firm in San Francisco, YCMNET Advisors, which has chosen an "aloha" approach to culture and clients. Here is a statement from YCMNET's president, Michael A. Yoshikami, concerning teamwork:

> *E lauhoe mai nâ wa`a,*
> Everybody paddle the canoes together;
> *i ke kâ, i ka hoe, i ke kâ;*
> bail and paddle, paddle and bail;
> *pae aku i ka `âina.*
> And the shore is reached.
> Pitch in with a will, everybody,
> and the work is done quickly.

In other words, teamwork wins. We agree.

All of our work rests on the integration of theory with practice. In *Investment Leadership*, our book on leadership and culture, we leaned heavily on the ideas of people like Jim Collins, Peter Senge, John Kotter, and Richard Barrett, pioneers in the area of values-based leadership. In this book, we take concepts and principles from Katie and Gay Hendricks of the Hendricks Institute and Kate Ludeman and Eddie Erlandson of Worth Ethic. The seven behaviors that we describe and apply to the investment industry were originally put forth in a book by Ludeman and Erlandson, called *Radical Change, Radical Results.*[3] (Ludeman and Erlandson, in turn, have credited the Hendricks Institute with many of the concepts detailed in their book.) We found these ideas for high-performing teams compelling and asked, "How would these ideas fare with investment professionals?" Our answer, after several years of working with investment teams around the world, is: remarkably well!

In brief, here are the seven behaviors demonstrated by top-performing teams:

1. **Curiosity:** Learning how to learn and learning on the run. In the face of feedback, top teams choose curiosity over defensiveness. The number-one characteristic of good leaders, according to the Center for Creative Leadership, is their capacity for learning, which is why we

start with this behavior. Learning agility is greatest when leaders are open to all feedback from all sources. Our experience with top investment firms supports this contention. Members of the best teams recognize when they are becoming defensive and know how to shift themselves back to an open and receptive attitude.

Example: Partners of a successful investment firm in Calgary had wrestled with ownership issues for years. The nature of the discussion invariably elicited defensive behavior from the senior team members (for example, partners protecting their own interests and being unwilling to consider the interests of the others). They had been unable to resolve their differences despite generally good rapport among the partners. Once the partners learned how to identify defensive behavior and shift to curiosity, and—importantly—once they committed to behaving this way during the discussions over ownership, they made new breakthroughs in resolving the issue.

2. **Accountability:** Taking 100 percent responsibility and making and keeping clear agreements. We cover this behavior next because it scores the highest ratings in our surveys of top investment firms; they all agree that the best leaders build cultures of accountability. However, doing so requires skill and a thorough understanding of the term *accountability*. Too many leaders operate from a "blame" mentality. To them, accountability means finding out who is to blame and getting those persons to own up to mistakes. Skillful accountability really means understanding the past—why mistakes happened—but then focusing on what each team member can do to improve future results. Too many firms operate from the "Apprentice" model of accountability (named after the Donald Trump television show, *The Apprentice*), in which the goal seems to be to point the finger at as many teammates as possible so that they look bad and get fired, leaving the finger-pointer the winner at the end. Not the ideal way to build team spirit! On the best teams, each person assumes 100 percent responsibility for the results that are being created.

   Example: John Rogers and Mellody Hobson at Ariel have built a great culture of accountability. Team members feel more responsible for achieving results than for explaining why results did not happen. When problems occur, team members ask themselves, "What was my role in creating this result?"

3. **Candor:** Telling the truth. Power and speed in decision making result from telling the whole truth. (Somewhat horrifyingly, a study from the University of Oklahoma concluded that one out of three business interactions involves a lie.[4]) We introduce this behavior early in the book, just as we do in offsite seminars and workshops, because it is absolutely fundamental to a team's speed and efficiency. Great leaders model courageous truth-telling. They understand the difference between facts and opinions and carefully apply this knowledge in their discussions. They also learn to hold their own opinions lightly, recognizing the difference between opinion and "truth." Further, the top teams know that each individual view is incomplete; by combining individuals' views, the clearest picture of reality emerges—and the team that sees reality the clearest is the winner (according to Jack Welch).[5] The best investment firms create an environment of open and candid communication in which each member contributes his or her own view, ensuring that all the facts are quickly put on the table so that decision making can be informed and rapid.

    Example: Michelle Seitz at William Blair has earned the respect and trust of her staff by being extremely candid. After taking over the job of CIO at the ripe old age of 35, she received rave reviews from the staff for her leadership. In no small way, her candor was responsible: "She gets the highest marks from me with regard to her open and honest communication with the department," wrote one of her direct reports.

4. **Authenticity:** Eliminating drama from the workplace. Candor leads to people getting real, and getting real can lead to conflict. Chapter 4 presents tools for resolving conflict and breaking free from limiting roles such as Victim, Villain, and Hero/Rescuer. Top leaders know that, to be effective, they must be genuine. Investment professionals are extremely perceptive and can spot a phony a mile away. Our experience shows that leaders who have learned to discard facades and can present themselves authentically reap huge rewards in staff productivity, trust, and loyalty.

    Example: Bill Lyons, CEO at American Century, displayed his authenticity when he assumed the top job: "I will invite people to see the man behind the curtain—I will not be afraid to openly show and express the entire range of human emotions, regardless of what their expectations of me, or my position, may be." Marie Arlt, COO at Analytic Investors, told us, "This material on authenticity has helped us more than any other you have presented."

5. **Awareness:** Using your mind/body intelligence by tapping fully into your emotional and intuitional intelligence. Top investment professionals use both logic and intuition in the decision-making process. To the extent that they "leave their emotions at the door," they limit their intuitive abilities. They also limit their abilities to read people and build trust. Bill Williams, trader for 35 years and author of the book, *Trading Chaos*, says, "Trading is almost all right hemispheres. It's all intuitive . . . you know what is the right trade without knowing how you know."[6]

   Example: Kim Redding, CEO of K.G. Redding & Associates, a real estate investment firm in Chicago, uses a highly intuitive approach to investment. Sometimes this approach is puzzling to the more linear-oriented thinkers in his shop. They say, "We don't know how he reaches his decisions." Nevertheless, they all acknowledge that his track record and accuracy are core reasons for the firm's success, and they have a high degree of confidence in his intuitive abilities. The ability to tap into all our resources for decision making is a powerful advantage in the investment world.

6. **Genius:** Discovering and aligning people with their true talents. Many leaders spend time and energy trying to shore up their own weaknesses and those of the staff. Truly effective investment professionals get good enough at basic skills and then leverage their natural areas of genius. Our experience with clients shows that the best firm leaders spend more than 75 percent of their time in their "genius" areas, delegating the tasks that fall outside to people who delight in and excel at those tasks.

   Example: Bob Turner at Turner Investment Partners, Charles Brandes at Brandes Investment Partners, and John Rogers at Ariel Capital Management share a passion—and genius—for investing. Each of them turned the operations of their firms over to a skilled manager, so that they could focus on the investment process. At Turner, for example, part of former president Steve Kneeley's (now with Ardmore Investments) bonus was based on his ability to allow the analysts and portfolio managers to focus on their investment work, without interruptions. Capital Group, widely known for its excellent culture, instituted The Associates Program (TAP), which allows new hires to move around in the company and thereby discover their true passion. The principle is simple: people will excel at what they love. And managing them will be relatively easy.

7. **Appreciation:** Expressing gratitude and building on the positive. Investment professionals are notorious for withholding praise and showering criticism on colleagues and staff. An inborn skill of investment leaders is critical analysis, so it's only natural they would use it in managing people. Research shows, though, that the most successful firms create a culture of appreciation, in which positive feedback outweighs negative in a ratio of 5:1. Focusing on the positive is a wise and proven strategy for success.

   Example: Jim Rudd, chairman of Ferguson Wellman Capital Management, has contributed his time and energy so generously to the United Way that it named its highest service award after him. This same positive spirit is evident in the firm's culture and its excellent results:

   > We serve more clients today than ever before. Our product offering, particularly to individuals and families, continues to see healthy demand. On the institutional side, we have brought in business as well but at a slower pace. Like all managers, we . . . lost some business in [2002]. The positive side to that story is that the new business easily outpaces any lost business and we expect this trend to continue.[7]

The value and efficacy of these seven behaviors are supported by a great deal of research in the field of psychology and organizational development. For example, the organization Human Synergistics has an elaborate and rich model for measuring culture in companies. They list 14 factors that contribute to a strong and constructive culture,[8] including:

- "Support and encourage others" (like our behavior of appreciation).
- Use "results-oriented accountability" (like our behavior of accountability).

- Foster "open communication" (like our behavior of candor).
- Derive "enjoyment from work" (like our behavior of genius).
- Cherish "feedback" (like our behavior of curiosity).

Consider also another heavily researched and often-quoted study, from the Gallup Organization, of what makes for a healthy workplace.[9] The researchers at Gallup boiled it all down to 12 questions, which they claim are the best test for whether or not you've created a healthy workplace. Here is the entire list:

1. Do I know what is expected of me at work?
2. Do I have the equipment and material I need to do my work right?
3. At work, do I have the opportunity to do what I do best every day?
4. In the last seven days, have I received recognition or praise for good work?
5. Does my supervisor or someone at work seem to care about me as a person?
6. Is there someone at work who encourages my development?
7. At work, do my opinions seem to count?
8. Does the mission/purpose of my company make me feel my work is important?
9. Are my co-workers committed to doing quality work?
10. Do I have a best friend at work?
11. In the last six months, have I talked to someone about my progress?
12. This last year, have I had the opportunities at work to learn and grow?[10]

Clearly, questions 3, 6, 11, and 12 address the behavior of genius: identifying and reinforcing a person's special talents. Question 4 addresses the behavior of appreciation. Accountability is picked up in question 9. The notion of curiosity and feedback is captured in several of the Gallup questions.

Another leading organization for leadership and development, The Lominger Group, has identified 67 competencies displayed by leaders, as well as 19 career-stallers. When we study this material, again we find that the seven behaviors we are presenting are captured in Lominger's extensive research. In fact, the first behavior that we describe is curiosity and openness to feedback (see Chapter 1), which they consider to be the most important of the 67 factors.

The preceding discussion is intended to reassure readers that there is extensive research to support the significance of the seven behaviors discussed in this book. From our direct work with investment organizations, we know that these seven pack the most punch. They are the seven most widely found in the top organizations. To put it the reverse way, when we work with or read about struggling investment firms, we find the opposite of these seven behaviors. We find behaviors like the following, which our friend and colleague, Kate Ludeman, calls "sludge" factors:

- Gossip
- Drama
- Defensiveness
- Disrespect
- Blame
- Entitlement
- Short-term focus
- Bureaucracy/territoriality
- Manipulation/politics
- Slow-moving/reactive
- Negative attitude

For each of these sludge factors, one of the seven behaviors is the antidote. For example, if a firm has developed a strong entitlement mentality—"we deserve high salaries, perks, and bonuses, regardless of our performance"—appreciation and accountability are key antidotes to learn and practice. If the firm is growing, and additional hires result in more politics, gossip, and corporate drama, then candor and authenticity are two excellent behaviors to learn and practice. You will find these cures to be true for the whole list.

What we know from our client work and research is that firms that approach a 40% sludge factor rating (on a scale of 0–100) are in serious danger of failing. This was the case with one financially successful firm that, in the eyes of the CEO, was growing too fast. Yes, they were making strong profits, but, to his credit, the CEO said, "The culture is disintegrating." When we performed a culture survey for this firm, the sludge factor was 36 percent. Since then, they have worked on the seven behaviors and improved that rating significantly. For the record, the best sludge-factor rating we've seen belongs to Brandes in San Diego. On the 0–100 scale, Brandes rated a mere 1 percent—nearly a perfect score. Our congratulations to Charles Brandes, Glenn Carlson, and Barry Gillman at Brandes, who have worked to create a nearly seamless operation where the results speak for themselves. Brandes's top-rated funds have grown so quickly that the firm has now capped nearly all of them. (Barry, the marketing director, has clients calling to say, "Please, let us put our additional money in *any* fund that is still open." How would you like *that* to be your firm's problem?!)

Okay, so what do you get if you practice these behaviors as an investment firm? What is the payoff? Where are the benefits? Here are some of the biggest benefits that Focus Consulting clients report from practicing and excelling at these behaviors:

- Greater speed and efficiency in decision making.
- Improved creativity. (One of our clients just won the Pinnacle Award for creativity and credits the use of these behaviors as part of the reason.)
- Lower turnover. (When people have the experience of being a member of a high-performing team, it is rare that another firm can lure them away, even for more money.)
- Higher run rates. (*Run rate* is the term we use for the amount of time investment professionals spend doing what they are paid to do. At top firms, this number is above 80 percent; some firms we've worked with hovered around 50 percent.)
- Less chance of ethical or legal breaches. (Firms that understand and practice accountability reduce their risk.)

In sum, firms that practice these behaviors operate at higher energy levels, have more passion and vitality in their work, and indulge in less politics, bureaucracy, gossip, and drama.

When Jim Dethmer and I present these behaviors to various investment groups around the world, we often get asked questions like, "Are we supposed to practice these behaviors—say, candor—with all of our business contacts? Clients and competitors alike?" The tone of this question usually suggests that it is not actually a question at all, but rather a statement: *You must be crazy to think that we're going to be open and revealing with everyone on Wall Street!* Good point. And, no, we do not encourage you to practice these behaviors with everyone. They are meant to allow you and your teammates to play on a different level from average firms. They are, however, based on the premise that all team members have made a conscious decision—that is, a willing and informed decision—to play by these rules of engagement.

The Prisoner's Dilemma, developed during the Cold War period, is a good experiential exercise to show why it is in everyone's best interest to cooperate rather than compete internally. The bottom line of that game is what experts call the strategy of "tit for tat." In other words, if all members of your team are willing to cooperate, then you should be, too. Everyone will benefit. But if one or more of the team members wants to game the system, then you need to protect yourself and play defensively. Here's one quick example where it would be professional suicide to practice one of our behaviors without an agreement from the leader and team: taking responsibility versus assigning blame. In top-performing teams, each member takes responsibility for her contribution to the outcome. So, if an investment goes south, everyone steps to the table and says, "Here's my part in it, and here's what I can do differently next time." Teams that operate using this guideline get the most out of post-mortems and learn quickly.

However, if you are on a team that worships at the altar of blame and finger-pointing, and, worse yet, where the boss does too, then watch out. (For a good example of this behavior, just watch *The Apprentice*, in which Trump summarily fires anyone who has the guts to say, "It was my fault.") Your sensible and productive behavior of taking responsibility will simply allow teammates to say, "See, I told you it wasn't my fault! It's *his* fault [fingers pointing at you]!" You'll read much more about accountability and how to do it right in Chapter 2.

The point here is a broader one: As you read about these seven behaviors, ask yourself two questions:

1. Is this the way my team plays the game?
2. If no, is there a good likelihood that they will convert to these behaviors?

Two of us at the Focus Consulting Group asked these very questions of old employers and left because the answer was no in both cases. When you play on a team where behaviors like trust, candor, and accountability are understood and embraced, two things happen: results improve and your quality of life goes way up. Oh, yes, a third thing happens as well: you reduce your legal expenses considerably. Warren Buffett knows this principle, and thus is comfortable evaluating the leaders of target-acquisition companies carefully and doing deals on a handshake. Trust-worthy, win/win partners are the only kind Buffett wants. He avoids the headaches and dangers by keeping the sharks out of his private swimming waters.

In addition to describing and applying these behaviors to investment situations, we also address the issue of investment personalities and how they relate to these seven behaviors. Based on the typical personality of an asset manager, some of the behaviors will come easier than others. Chapter 9 outlines the strengths and weakness of investment managers in this regard.

Finally (by popular demand), we also cover another key concept, decision rights. We include this chapter because our approach to decision rights has gained an enormous amount of traction and acceptance with our clients. The principle is simple. Establish clear guidelines for each decision, including:

- Who has decision rights?
- What method of decision making will be used?

When leaders and teams take the time to get clear on these questions, the entire team settles down because each team member understands his or her role in the decision-making process. Without this clarity, meetings can drag on endlessly and team morale sags.

A final thought before we turn you loose on exploring what makes a great team and great team players. One of our great joys in working with professional investors occurs when we receive notes like the following from serious, tough portfolio managers. Jerome, who was the biggest skeptic in the room when his firm engaged us to help with teamwork and culture, wrote:

Just a quick note on why your meetings have stuck with me: You both seem to understand the importance of the "big picture." I especially liked the fact that you mixed in family relationships with the message. My wife and I have always gotten along well, but my communication skills have picked up after our meetings. The other significant point that I have come to realize is that we get along so well and function so well as a team because my wife and I are EQUALLY committed. Regardless of who fits where on the commitment scale, it is difficult to accomplish anything without matched commitment levels. I was, of course, reminded of this again yesterday as I took my four-year-old out for her first lesson on a bike without training wheels . . . . She, at least, remains committed to the IDEA of riding without training wheels!

All the principles in this book apply to both personal and professional relationships. The key, as Jerome correctly noted, is commitment. Whether in business concerns or family matters, conscious commitment is essential.

That said, we invite you to commit yourself to keeping an open mind and heart as you read this material. It's our pleasure to share it with you.

CHAPTER 1

Investment Leadership

Building a Winning Culture for Long-Term Success

Jim Ware

Over the long term, culture dominates.
—Charles Ellis, Greenwich Associates

Our previous book, *Investment Leadership: Building a Winning Culture for Long-Term Success*,[1] examined the elements of leadership that significantly contribute to the sustainable success of an investment firm. The concepts and research presented in that book set a context for this present book, which delves more deeply into the specific behaviors of top-performing teams. *Investment Leadership* was written in the aftermath of a 17-year bull market. During that time, it was relatively easy for an investment firm—any investment firm—to prosper. In fact, during a recent presentation to a group of Chartered Financial Analysts (CFAs) in New York, I flippantly remarked, "During the '90s, Forrest Gump could have managed a successful investment firm." One audience member, without missing a beat, responded, "He did!"

The prevailing attitude at that time seemed to be, "Give us some individuals with solid investment talent and we can win." (Or, to paraphrase the line from *Blazing Saddles*, "We don't need no stinking culture!") *Investment Leadership* chronicled the fortunes of a semifictitious firm called Allstar, which had grown to $40 billion in assets by the turn of the twenty-first century, only to fail completely three years later (and not, by the way, because of legal or talent problems). In our view, Allstar failed because of leadership and culture issues. To support this contention, it was important that we provide lots of data on leadership and culture—so we did.

In sharp contrast to the overconfident and somewhat naïve view of leadership during the 1990s ("Anyone can manage an investment firm"), we are finding now that leadership, culture, and teamwork are top priorities for investment firms. We no longer get quizzical looks and furrowed brows from CEOs asking, "Why would we worry about those soft issues?" Even the thickest-skinned, toughest-minded investment leader understands that the so-called soft skills are critical in attracting, retaining, and motivating talent. These leaders also know that optimal use of talent is the key to success in investment firms. (One Canadian CEO whose firm suffered from high turnover committed the ultimate Freudian slip when he said, "We do attack and retrain the best talent!")

The following is a quick review of the key concepts from *Investment Leadership*. If you have read our first book and do not want a review, skip this chapter and go directly to Chapter 2.

THE CULTURE THING

To begin with, what is *culture*? We use the following working definition:

> The beliefs, values, and behaviors that differentiate one organization from another.

Because leaders have the most influence over beliefs, values, and behaviors in a firm, they have the most influence over culture. Anyone who has recently changed investment firms can appreciate this difference. From the physical layout of the firm's offices, to the way decisions are made, to the beliefs about how markets work, firms differ. Gary Brinson used to compare investment cultures to world religions: Each may be valid in its own way or sphere, but they are very different from one another.[2] We agree that there are many ways to skin the investment-culture cat, but we have found some guiding principles that are common to the best firms.

First, though, let's examine some evidence that highlights the importance of leadership and culture in the industry. The following list shows the factors that contribute most to investment employee satisfaction and commitment. In the war for talent, this information is critical. The best firms attract, retain, and motivate top talent. How do they do it? Here are the key factors:[3]

1. Leadership credibility and trust   84.8%
2. Organizational culture and purpose   69.6
3. Opportunity for growth and development   50.0
4. Challenging, meaningful work   50.0
5. Total compensation   50.0
6. Relationships with co-workers, customers   39.1
7. Work recognition   39.1
8. Quality of life/work balance   28.3
9. Ownership   24.4

Notice that leadership and culture are the top two factors. Our view of this data is based on three important connections that top investment firms establish and foster:

1. A connection of trust among leaders, professionals, and clients. When trust and respect exist in a culture, individuals make deeper connections with one another because f̲

.at
ir-
g-
le
t,
t-

s.

Factors 3 and 4 in the preceding list relate to this connection. People feel and perform best when they exercise and develop their own special gifts.

In short, these three connections can be thought of as "above" (mission and higher purpose), "around" (with trusting relationships), and "inside" (with their own unique talents). Good leaders create cultures in which all three connections are developed and strengthened.

These basic concepts are necessary, but how does one think about culture in a practical way? What model is helpful in understanding how to measure and shape culture? We use the causative model shown in Figure 1.1 to understand the key elements.

In consulting work, we at the Focus Consulting Group start with results. This word is carefully chosen: not *vision* or *mission*, but *results*. Why? Because some firms may quibble over whether they even have a vision or mission or goal statement—but all firms, every day, produce results. The word *results* eliminates any hiding place. The question thus becomes, "Are you producing the results you want?" Therefore, we start by investigating what success looks like and how we would know if we achieved it. In short, what results are we aiming for?

In this process, we encourage leaders to be as inclusive as possible in creating a document that describes the firm's successful future state. The

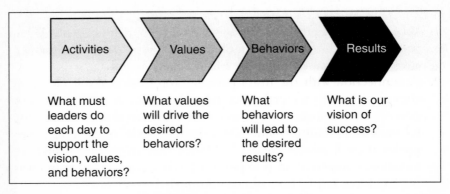

FIGURE 1.1 Causative model.

range of possible inclusion levels goes from the CEO crafting the document personally and telling everyone what it contains, to the leadership team starting with a blank sheet of paper and creating the document with the help and input of the entire staff. (Obviously, this is harder to do for UBS than for Analytic Investors.)

Backing up a step from results, we then discuss which behaviors will lead to the desired results, and which values will drive those behaviors. We provide a process by which investment firms can identify, define, and implement (*behavioralize*) values. For example, a company can create a list of measurable behaviors that are then used as a scorecard to track progress.

To summarize, the causal chain is that *beliefs* underlie *values*, which drive *behaviors*, which in turn create *results*.

In this context, what does the term *activity* mean? Underlying values, behaviors, and results is the need for leaders—and employees—to constantly reinforce key activities so that employees clearly see that "walking the talk" matters. When discussing these cultural issues with investment leaders, I always ask for an example of a top performer being dismissed because he or she didn't fit with the culture. From the top firms, I invariably get concrete examples of just that, usually along with an admission that those decisions are some of the toughest they ever have to make. Leaders at top firms are clear about vision, values, and behaviors and are relentless about reinforcing them by creating experiences that recognize and reward them. For example, American Century in Kansas City devotes an entire day to celebrating the five employees who best exemplify the company's five values.

With all this emphasis on vision and values, what other evidence exists (aside from the fact that employees like good leaders and strong cultures) proving that values and vision contribute to superior results? How do we link culture work to the bottom line? We offer the work of Collins and Porras in *Built to Last*[4] as strong evidence that firms that pay careful attention to culture outperform their competition over the long term. In fact, the 18 firms that Collins and Porras identified as superior companies outperformed the 18 comparison companies by a wide margin. For example, $1 invested in the superior companies during the period 1926–1990 grew to $6,356, versus $415 for the comparison companies. (For the record, the superior companies were not chosen based on stock appreciation, but rather on factors such as reputation and quality of products and services.)

With this huge difference in stock performance, though, it makes excellent sense to ask if there were consistent differences between the two groups of companies. Collins and Porras found 21 factors that explained the difference between "great" and "good." Six of the most telling factors involved leadership and culture. We have extended Collins's and Porras's work into the investment community and measured these same factors.

In what follows, we describe the six key factors and present the data for the original *Built to Last* superior (BTL) and comparison companies. We also include our own data from 35 well-known investment firms. The range of scores is from +1 to –1, with zero being a middle rating. In each case, BTL companies scored higher than the comparison companies. Investment firms (average of 35 well-known firms as self-rated by members of their leadership teams) tended to score in between these two groups. This makes intuitive sense, as the investment firm sample combined top companies, such as Capital Group, Goldman Sachs, and William Blair, with firms that fit the description of comparison companies (that is, average performers). In our experience, top investment firms score well on the following six factors.

CULTURE SUCCESS FACTOR 1: CLARITY OF VALUES AND VISION

The company has identified and articulated core values and a vision and uses them as a source of guidance (see Table 1.1).

Top-performing companies worship at the altar of clarity. They have carefully identified and defined the results they want and the values, beliefs, and behaviors that will help them achieve those results. The very best firms make this process as inclusive as possible. They invite in all the key stakeholders so that each person's voice will be recognized. In this way, they build a high degree of ownership in the firm's vision and values. Investment professionals want to work with organizations that have strong cultures and purpose. A necessary ingredient in such a culture is

TABLE 1.1 Scores for "Clarity of Values and Vision"

BTL Companies	Comparison Companies	35 Investment Firms
.78	−.11	.42

conscious focus on and precision in the firm's values and vision. In the case of investment firms, part of that precision extends to the description of the investment process. The best firms have great clarity about the investment process itself and where each employee adds value.

The data in Table 1.1 shows that the average investment firm rated itself significantly behind the BTL companies. Note that the sample of 35 investment firms included stellar performers such as Capital Group, as well as companies that were, by their own admission, struggling. The message to take away is clear: There is great opportunity for most investment firms to improve their scores in this area.

There is good news here. Our experience in talking with leaders from around the globe reveals that the prevailing viewpoint as to culture is shifting. Increasingly, investment leaders are acknowledging the role of culture in performance. Leaders are beginning to understand the difference between working "in" the business (blocking and tackling on the field) and working "on" the business (going up to the skybox and observing). A relatively small investment of time (typically two days) at a carefully facilitated offsite meeting can translate into enormous competitive advantages. (We have yet to hear from a team after an offsite, "Sorry, but that just wasn't worth the time invested." Invariably, it's just the opposite: "We should have done this years ago!")

CULTURE SUCCESS FACTOR 2: CONSISTENCY OF VALUES AND VISION

The values and vision described have undergone little change since inception (see Table 1.2).

So your firm has established values and a vision—good! The question then becomes: Have the vision and values been in place for a while, or do they change like the latest fashion fad? Consider two extreme cases.

TABLE 1.2 Scores for "Consistency of Values and Vision"

BTL Companies	Comparison Companies	35 Investment Firms
.67	−.89	.34

First is the building of the Sears Financial Network. Remember the so-called socks-and-stocks experiment? The leaders of Sears put forth a vision to build a financial network that would allow consumers to take care of all their financial needs under one roof; a financial supermarket, if you will. Almost a decade in the making during the 1980s, the whole enterprise had been dismantled by the early 1990s. Hence, a poor score for consistency of values and vision.

Consider the opposite example, just down the street from the Sears Tower. John Rogers started Ariel Capital Management in the mid-1980s with a laser-like focus on becoming the premier name in small and mid-cap value investing. Over the next 20 years, Rogers grew the company from a few hundred million under management to the $20-billion, top-rated firm that it is today. The firm's mascot is the tortoise and its motto is "Slow and steady wins the race." Everything in the firm proclaims "Focus!" Ariel is vivid testimony to the power of consistency and focus.

Our recommendation concerning the consistency factor is simple: Do it right the first time. Most visions and values shift because the process originally used to develop them was not thorough. If you take the process seriously and dig deep, you won't need to revisit the vision and values a year later to redo the process. The old carpenter's rule of "measure twice, cut once" applies here.

CULTURE SUCCESS FACTOR 3: ALIGNMENT WITH VALUES AND VISION

The vision and values are "alive" in the company (see Table 1.3).

Factor 3 could be called the "walk-the-talk" factor. Do the leaders and staff really embody the values and embrace the vision? We worked with a $60-billion, buy-side organization that had completed work on Factors 1 and 2. Values and vision were identified and printed on wall hangings and paperweights, and they had been in place for at least six years. The prob-

TABLE 1.3   Scores for "Alignment with Values and Vision"

BTL Companies	Comparison Companies	35 Investment Firms
.72	−.20	.22

lem came in walking the talk. We made it a practice, every day while we were on site, to ask several employees: "What are the guiding vision and core values of this firm?" Of the 280 employees, exactly one could answer the question with conviction and accuracy. She was the director of human resources, whom I later found out had crafted the statements.

Built to Last companies score very high on this factor. Employees know the core values and vision and reflect them in their actions. The average score for investment firms (.22) suggests that there are great opportunities for them to strengthen their cultures. There are several effective ways to do this. Leaders' reclarification of and recommitment to the vision and values can have a quick and powerful impact on the staff. Employees watch leaders like Fed watchers eye Alan Greenspan. Every single word and gesture is analyzed and critiqued. Smart leaders understand this human tendency and make sure that signals from the senior team are clear and aligned.

A second technique involves recognizing and rewarding staff who walk the talk. American Century's recognition day celebrates staff members who have shown exemplary behavior involving values. For example, each year one employee is nominated by colleagues for being the most innovative. He or she receives money and public recognition for this contribution.

Firms that have clearly identified their values and vision and are successfully walking the talk are well on their way to Success Factor 4, a strong culture.

CULTURE SUCCESS FACTOR 4: STRONG CULTURE

The firm's culture is well defined and "binary"; that is, some people love it and others hate it (see Table 1.4).

Even the best of the best, the *Built to Last* companies, only muster a score of .44 on this factor. It's not easy to build a strong culture. Firms that

TABLE 1.4 Scores for "Strong Culture"

BTL Companies	Comparison Companies	35 Investment Firms
.44	−.33	.21

rate highly here are characterized by great pride in their products and services, elitism ("we're the best"), and a binary nature. *Binary* means that some people would love it and some would hate it. In the investment world, Vanguard is an excellent example. Founded by Jack Bogle, Vanguard has a strong nautical theme running through its culture. (The firm's name itself comes from the winning ship in a naval battle between Lord Nelson and Napoleon's forces; the French surrendered to the *HMS Vanguard* in 1798.) The buildings at the headquarters are named after sailing vessels. There are paintings of ships on the walls. The employees are called the "crew." The cafeteria is called the "galley." The bathrooms are the "head." If a crew member is missing, one almost expects to hear, "Man overboard!" The director of corporate communications once told me that his neighbors tease him about working for the "cult company." The comments neither surprise nor upset him. He acknowledges the cult-like nature of Vanguard, that is, its strong culture. He is proud of the firm.

What does one do to achieve strong culture? Factors 1 through 3 are critical and cannot be skipped over; no shortcuts there. Assuming that leaders are serious about establishing a strong culture, the critical step for Factor 4 is aligning hiring practices, incentives, and performance management processes with values and vision. Staff members must see evidence that employees are hired, promoted, recognized, and rewarded based on their conformity with the firm's cultural norms. ATB Financial in Calgary is so serious about hiring good "fits" that they actually have a page of recruiting material listing the characteristics of people who should *not* work for the company! Sheldon Dyck, ATB's investment leader, takes culture seriously and can offer up stories in which a top performer was dismissed from the firm because she or he wasn't a cultural fit. Nothing sends a clearer message to the troops that culture matters than the dismissal of a top producer. Firing a star player sends the message that leaders care not only about results, but also about how they are achieved.

CULTURE SUCCESS FACTOR 5: CULTURAL INDOCTRINATION

New hires are informed and educated about the culture of the company (see Table 1.5).

Built to Last firms far outscore comparison companies and the average investment firm in the area of indoctrination. Obviously, indoctrination can happen only in firms with fairly strong cultures. After all, how would you indoctrinate someone into an amorphous culture? There would be no clear guidelines or norms in such an environment. Hence, Factors 1 through 4 must be tended to before a firm can tackle this fifth step. Firms commonly make the error of ignoring this area, despite having done the hard work of creating a strong culture. Rather than carefully managing the process of training new hires, leaders often incorrectly assume that rookies will learn by osmosis.

Top investment firms do not take this chance. They establish formal and effective training programs that quickly get the new hires acculturated. A key consideration for any new hire is, "How do I succeed in this organization?" The orientation program should address this issue. What is expected from employees? What factors translate into promotions, pay increases, and bonuses? The same is true with new leaders. Top firms have a careful assimilation program for new leaders, which allows these individuals to get up and running quickly.

Ariel Capital takes the indoctrination process extremely seriously. Its "Ambassador" program concentrates on the new recruits' first 100 days. In that time, the new hires learn the firm's values, vision, product offerings, performance results, strategies, investment philosophies, and so on. At the end of 100 days, each new hire knows enough to be considered an "ambassador of the company." Capital Group also provides clear cultural guidelines. Its TAP program for new recruits is one such vehicle. David

TABLE 1.5   Scores for "Cultural Indoctrination"

BTL Companies	Comparison Companies	35 Investment Firms
.61	−.39	.17

Fisher at Capital Group believes that "culture is our only competitive advantage" and plans accordingly.

CULTURE SUCCESS FACTOR 6: SUCCESSION OF LEADERSHIP

The company has a history of careful succession planning and formal leadership grooming (see Table 1.6).

Leadership drives culture, so the development of leaders is critical to building a winning culture. Even with a carefully planned and skillfully facilitated new-leader assimilation process, the sharpest, most willing learners still require months to get the feel of a new culture. Worse yet, many new leaders don't even try to understand what they've inherited. Rather, they resort to bringing in people from their old firms in an effort to reproduce that old culture. This move can work if the firms' cultures happen to be very similar, but most are not. The evidence is clear: Outside leaders are disastrous when they ignore the existing culture. Looking more broadly, research and statistics indicate that many mergers, acquisitions, and new regimes fail when inadequate attention is given to the viability of combining cultures.

Several years ago I watched as a buy-side investment firm brought in a new outside chief investment officer (CIO). For the next several years, the firm suffered relatively high turnover. Significant time and money were lost as people tried to figure out the new way of doing things. Key players eventually became frustrated and left. After a few years, the firm finally stabilized at a mediocre level of performance. Then, amazingly enough, the whole cycle recurred when the CIO was tapped for another

TABLE 1.6 Scores for "Succession of Leadership"

BTL Companies	Comparison Companies	35 Investment Firms
.33	−.39	−.06

assignment in the parent company! Although he had had six years to find his successor, the CIO had not groomed a replacement, so, once again, the firm brought in yet another new CIO from the outside. The same turmoil ensued, but to an even greater extent. The most notable example of the talent drain occurred when a derivatives trader left two weeks before the end of the year. All his colleagues reminded him that if he could just "gut it out" until December 31, he would be entitled to a sizeable bonus. His response? "It's not worth it." And he left, with his bonus still on the table. Basically, he walked away from a Mercedes because the environment was so bad that he couldn't take it one more day.

Most investment firms traditionally have followed the tribal method of leadership. Each tribe—fixed income, equities, real estate, privates, etc.—establishes its own rituals and ways of doing things. Then, as if at a secret midnight ceremony, these rituals are passed down to the next generation, along with secret handshakes. Today's top-performing firms, however, are beginning to look at a more formal approach to succession. With culture in mind, we recommend designing leadership development programs based on the unique vision, values, strategies, and investment philosophy of the particular company. We have helped firms develop leadership programs that include "soft" skills such as:

- Managing difficult employees (i.e., "stars").
- Interviewing and hiring for both skills and culture fit.
- Handling performance management, especially delivering tough reviews effectively.
- Resolving conflicts, including techniques for clearing the air on a regular basis.
- Giving and receiving feedback, on a regular basis, skillfully, with both candor and tact.
- Embodying accountability and integrity (defining and operationalizing these key concepts).
- Coaching and mentoring (developing and assessing the rising talent in a firm).
- Building trust (recognizing that success rests on the "three legs of trust: congruence, competence, and caring"[5]).

- Fostering teamwork (defining roles, responsibilities, and critical guidelines).
- Demonstrating emotional intelligence (developing self-awareness and relationship skills).

The last skill, emotional intelligence, was made famous by Daniel Goleman in his book of the same title.[6] This skill has been identified by reputable organizations (including the Center for Creative Leadership) as the key leadership skill yielding success, even ahead of IQ or experience. Obviously it's critically important . . . but what is it? Emotional intelligence has four basic elements:

1. The ability to identify one's feelings and behaviors (self-awareness).
2. The ability to manage one's internal state (self-control).
3. The ability to recognize and understand others' emotional states (empathy).
4. The ability to manage skillfully one's relationships with others (rapport).

CULTURE FOR COMPETITIVE ADVANTAGE

To recap, the six culture factors discussed in this chapter are powerful and effective steps that the best investment firms have taken to secure a competitive advantage. As David Fisher noted, and other leaders of top firms agree, "Culture is our only competitive advantage."[7]

The formula is simple, but not easy to implement. For one thing, success requires a deep commitment at all levels of an organization. For this reason, Focus Consulting Group uses a "Readiness Survey" with firms that are considering a culture change. Typically we discuss leadership and culture with the key opinion leaders and then distribute a survey that asks questions such as:

- Does the process make sense to you?
- Do the facilitators seem capable?
- Is the level of urgency in your organization high enough?
- Are trust levels sufficient to make real progress?

- Is senior leadership committed to the change process?
- Is senior leadership capable of leading us through the change?

If the responses to these questions are lukewarm, typically the level of commitment from participants will also be lukewarm. In these cases, we recommend postponing the process and dealing with the obstacles.

PRACTICAL APPLICATIONS

For the more "hands-on"-oriented readers, let me give a few illustrations of how the Focus Consulting Group has applied these concepts with clients.

A large, East Coast money manager with a very strong performance record is planning to double the assets it has under management in the next three years. The senior management team's concern is keeping the company's successful culture *pure*. They obviously don't want to wreck their winning formula. They asked us to analyze their current organization and design training on how to hire an excellent fit for their culture. This work involved clarifying the outstanding features of the firm's current culture and developing an interview process that specifically incorporated these features into questions for candidates. The outcome of this customized, tighter interview process is objective rankings as to how well each candidate will fit with the existing culture.

Another practical application of leadership and culture work is designing a customized leadership development program. Recognizing that they were heavily dependent on the tribal approach to leadership development, one firm that Focus Consulting Group works with asked us to design a more formal program that would fit with its current environment. The process again started with analyzing the company's culture, defining it, and leveraging the talents and strengths of leaders who were currently excelling in that environment. The practical outcome of this assignment was a definition of what it means to be an effective leader at that particular firm. Formal training and executive coaching (including 360-degree feedback) were used to drive home the desired attitudes and behaviors.

The result was a good fit between leadership and culture. Leaders reinforce the appropriate beliefs, values, and behaviors. When done skill-fully, this process also addresses the succession issue, as internal leaders are prepared to take over when senior people leave. Both the evidence and our experience clearly support the case for home-grown leadership.

A third application addresses mergers and acquisitions. A large global investment firm asked us to help define and integrate the cultures of four different firms that it had acquired. This process involved facili-tating a discussion between key opinion leaders of the newly formed enti-ty and gaining agreement on the new vision and values. The acquirer's strategy and desire was to capture the best practices of each separate firm and leverage them for use by the new entity. A different strategy, employed by parent companies such as AMG, Old Mutual, and Conver-gent Capital, is to acquire asset management firms and leave the existing cultures intact. A blend of the two strategies is employed by NatCan in Montreal, where three distinct asset management groups have defined their own separate cultures but collectively agree on "meta-values" at the parent-company level.

CONCLUSION

Leadership drives culture, which in turn drives investment performance. Building a strong culture requires leaders to work "on" the business, as opposed to their normal task of working "in" the business. Leaders must step away long enough to deeply consider and identify a clear vision and strong values. They must then walk the talk and reward staff members who do the same.

Our research shows that a huge opportunity exists for investment firms to differentiate themselves from the pack by strengthening their cultures. Specific areas on which to focus are:

- Clearly define vision and values.
- Communicate the vision and values and reward behaviors that reflect and promote them.
- Hire for cultural fit.
- Indoctrinate new hires and new leaders carefully and thoroughly.

- Promote and compensate using a cultural-factors approach.
- Develop strong leaders from within the firm via formal training and coaching.

The aim of *High Performing Investment Teams* is to describe and teach the seven key behaviors that we find in top firms. These behaviors are woven into the fabric of a top firm's culture and day-to-day activities. From the newly hired receptionist to the CEO of 10 years' standing, each professional at the firm understands and lives these behaviors, because each employee understands why these behaviors are important to the long-term success of the firm.

CHAPTER 2

Curiosity
Learning How to Learn

Jim Ware

Ours is a scary, competitive business. If you don't learn, you're dead.
—Peter Bernstein

The Canadian-based firm had a problem. Despite financial success and general good will among the partners, there was a chasm between the junior and senior partners that was threatening the company's success. The problem was one we often see in privately held money management firms: ownership. In this case, nine partners were owners, with the three founding partners holding the largest portion (more than 50 percent). The line had been drawn in the sand and the positions for each faction were predictable: The founders claimed that they deserved the lion's share for taking the early risk and providing a platform for the young Turks to perform on. The young Turks claimed that they were now bringing in most of the new business and should be rewarded accordingly. The battle for ownership had been raging for nearly two years, with no discernible progress or change on either side. The effect that the argument was having on team morale was becoming pronounced, with several young Turks beginning to mutter about splitting off and starting their own firm. In our view, that action was likely to be lose/lose for all involved.

We'll return to the Canadian firm's dilemma shortly, but first let me state that the solution to such issues lies in the first high-performance behavior: learning agility. We start with learning agility because in large part it is a prerequisite for all the other behaviors. *Learning agility* means being open and receptive to new ideas and to feedback.

Ask any investment team members whether they know how to learn and they will undoubtedly answer, "Yes, of course. To win in this business, we have to be able to learn."

Unfortunately, most of them are not in fact skilled at learning. "What?!" you say. "We have some of the best and the brightest people in the world on our investment staff!" Fair enough—but don't confuse raw intelligence with learning. The former, as measured by IQ and academic scores, is a necessary but not sufficient condition for investment success. Chris Argyris, a Harvard Business School professor, in a classic article entitled, "Teaching Smart People How to Learn," wrote:

> Many professionals are almost always successful at what they do, [and therefore] rarely experience failure. And because they have rarely failed, they have never learned how to learn from failure . . . . [I]nstead, they become defensive, screen out criticism, and put the "blame" on anyone and everyone but themselves. In short, their ability to learn shuts down precisely at the moment they need it the most.[1]

Getting defensive and blaming others are common human behaviors, especially in the face of feedback. What was your reaction the last time your manager said, "Can you come into my office? I'd like to give you a little feedback"? Probably something other than: "Fantastic! What a great learning opportunity!" It's natural to get defensive in these situations; even professionals on high-performing teams do it. But here's the difference. Members of high-performing teams don't stay defensive for very long. They have learned to watch their own behavior—and that of their teammates—so that they can identify the early warning signs of defensiveness, a posture that shuts down learning.

DO YOU KNOW IF YOU'RE DEFENSIVE?

We work with investment teams, week in and week out, and always ask them early on: "Do you know how to tell if you're getting defensive?" In response, we typically get blank stares. People understand the concept of defensiveness very well, but they're not aware of their own physical and mental signals of defensiveness. In our experience, the very best investment professionals know when they are getting defensive and know how to shift back to being open and curious. As a tool for teams that are first learning these techniques, we provide a list of common indicators of defensiveness (the negative numbers) and curiosity (the positive numbers) on a Defensiveness Scale (see Figure 2.1).

Team members use this information to get familiar with how defensiveness appears in themselves and their teammates. Again, the goal is not to eliminate defensiveness; rather, the intent is to spot it and make a conscious choice to shift back into an attitude of openness and curiosity. Notice that we view this choice as a legitimate option: at any given moment, we can choose to remain defensive or move back to a different attitude.

To summarize, then, the three key behaviors of high-performing teams concerning reactions to feedback are:

1. Recognizing the signs of defensiveness (for example, tight throat, clenched stomach, eye roll, thoughts such as, "No, you're wrong.").
2. Choosing to shift back to openness and genuine curiosity. *Note:* Our experience with investment professionals is that this process works much better when this step is presented as a real choice, rather than a command. Investment professionals tend to get even more resistant when ordered to do something. Thus, we always phrase the question as follows: "Do you *want* to shift back to being curious?"

   If the response or choice is, "No," our advice is to end the discussion until the defensive person chooses to change his or her attitude. Our experience shows that very little constructive work or problem solving takes place when one or more team members is defensive.
3. Shifting from a defensive and closed attitude to a posture of openness and curiosity. In our years of working with investment professionals (any professionals, for that matter), we have encountered only a handful who initially have a good answer to the question, "What are some reliable things you can do to shift yourself from being closed and defensive to being open and receptive?" This is an important question. Every top-performing team member should have considered

The Key Transition Action: Choose Curiosity over Defending

(+10) Implement (plan action, request support for follow-up).

(+9) Feel and show a genuine enthusiasm about the possibilities.

(+8) Think out loud, making new associations about the issue.

(+7) Take full responsibility for the issue and the results.

(+6) Request information and examples about the issue.

(+5) Openly wonder about your role in creating the issue.

(+4) Express appreciation for the messenger and the message, regardless of delivery.

(+3) Listen generously (paraphrase others' points without interjecting your own).

(+2) Express genuine curiosity about the issue. Genuinely wonder about the issue with an open body position.

(+1) Look interested; breathe; demonstrate an open posture.

Defensiveness: Low Curiosity and Low Learning

(–1) DIRECT: Ask about the speaker's intention in bringing up this situation.
INDIRECT: Show polite interest, while inwardly clinging to your opinions.

(–2) DIRECT: Point out that the other person seems to be missing some information.
INDIRECT: Feel confused. Withdraw.

(–3) DIRECT: Explain how the person has misperceived the situation; provide a lot of supporting details to make sure they understand.
INDIRECT: Feel misunderstood and unappreciated for your efforts. Worry about how you're perceived, instead of taking action.

(–4) DIRECT: Interrupt. Then give a different perspective.
INDIRECT: Get silent and still; provide cryptic answers and act as if you feel put upon.

(–5) DIRECT: Interpret what the person says as an attack.
INDIRECT: Criticize the way the person delivers the message by thinking you'd feel less defensive, if only they had spoken to you more respectfully.

(–6) DIRECT: Provide an animated and long-winded justification for your behavior and why you're right and the other person is wrong.
INDIRECT: Knock something over, drop things, spill a cup of coffee. Nonverbal displays of anger, irritation, and exasperation.

(–7) DIRECT: Communicate with a tone of righteous indignation; demand evidence in a hostile manner.
INDIRECT: Get edgy, sharp, brusque, snappy, or nonverbally show your frustration in some other obvious way.

(–8) DIRECT: Blame someone or something else.
INDIRECT: Pretend you agree when you don't.

(–9) DIRECT: Attack or threaten the messenger, verbally or otherwise.
INDIRECT: Commit to do something when you don't plan to do it or don't have the time or resources to do it.

(–10) DIRECT: Create an uproar by making an abrupt departure.
INDIRECT: After you leave the meeting, complain to others about people or decisions; talk critically about people who aren't in the room; gossip.

FIGURE 2.1 Defensiveness Scale.

and answered this question. (Imagine a professional golfer who, when asked, "What do you do when you are playing poorly and need to get back on track?" responds, "Gee, I don't know. I never thought about it.")

Investment teams that aspire to be top-notch learners have developed reliable ways for team members to shift back to an attitude of curiosity. Here are some examples of *shift-moves* from top teams:

- **Move.** A simple technique for shifting out of defensiveness is to get up and do some physical activity—stand up, walk around, shake your arms out, rotate your neck. You can't stay defensive when you are moving. Simon Yates, Managing Director of Equity Derivatives at Credit Suisse First Boston, says that when his traders get nervous or defensive, he tells them, "Get off the desk. Go for a workout, or go sit in the park for an hour."
- **Breathe.** Another remarkably simple technique is to practice deep breathing. The Menninger Clinic has determined that nearly 90 percent of Americans breathe incorrectly. Instead of breathing fully, allowing the belly to expand, we tend to take short, upper-chest breaths that actually trigger the fight-or-flight response. This innate reaction tells your brain to pump adrenaline into your system, thus physically priming you for aggressive or evasive action—the direct opposite of a calming effect. Deep breathing triggers the release of a counteracting neurotransmitter that calms the mind and body and restores physical equilibrium. Phil Jackson, coach of the Bulls and Lakers basketball teams, once told us that he instructs all his players on proper breathing techniques. Why? Because when the pressure is on, "breathing is everything," he said.
- **Listen.** This technique works very well if you can put aside your own arguments and make understanding of the other person's position your sole mission. Very few people do this well. Our natural inclination is to immediately evaluate a person's position, either agreeing with it or disagreeing and mentally marshalling counter-arguments. Listening can be a powerful shift-move if you can train yourself to listen with genuine curiosity—what we sometimes call

naïve listening. Again, make it your goal to fully understand the other person's perspective without evaluating its merit.

- **Question.** The key to this shift-move is to stop your defensive reaction midstream and ask a question that genuinely interests you. For example, a great question at almost any point in a discussion is, "What can I learn from this that I don't already know?"

These four shift-moves have proved useful to many of our clients, but the goal is to find ones that work for you. For example, one partner with the New Dimensions Fund in San Diego said that his best shift-move was humor. When feeling defensive, he often could use self-effacing humor to get himself and others laughing. This technique transformed the energy from angry or fearful and heavy to joyful and light. We have identified 12 shift-moves that work well for individuals at Focus Consulting, but the point is to discover what works for you.

ABOVE OR BELOW THE LINE?

To promote the topic of top-notch learning in a practical way, we find the following simple terminology useful. We call a state of openness and curiosity being *above the line* and that of closed defensiveness being *below the line,* thereby playing with catchy language that turns up in the daily conversations of teams we work with. The principles are straightforward (see also Figure 2.2):

- Top investment teams make a conscious commitment to one another to play above the line.
- Top investment teams spend most of their time above the line.
- When an individual or several members of a team go below the line, little constructive decision making will follow. (So, either shift or dismiss the meeting.)

Repeated instances of a team member refusing to shift from defensive to curious are grounds for dismissal. This is pretty clear evidence of a bad fit with the firm's culture and aims.

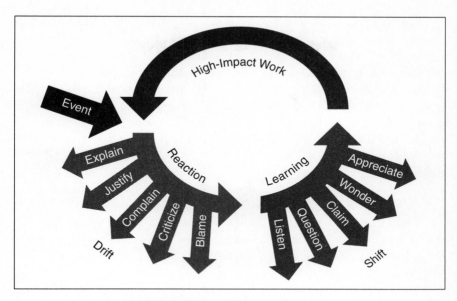

FIGURE 2.2   Feedback to learning.

THE ACID TEST: UNTYING THE GORDIAN KNOT IN CANADA

We now return to the firm in Canada with the ownership issue, whose predicament opened this chapter. We believe that they achieved their breakthrough once they understood and practiced the notion of playing (behaving) above the line. When we met with this group of partners, we spent the first several hours discussing this principle of learning agility, along with some of the other behaviors discussed in subsequent chapters. The mindset of a group—its rules of engagement—is critically important to its ability to solve problems. We like to quote Einstein in this regard: "A problem cannot be solved by the same consciousness that created it." Whenever we work with investment teams, we devote the first portion of our time together to creating a shift in mindset, one that we believe promotes the most productive and creative solutions. With the Canadian owners, we spent time explaining what "above the line" meant, then practicing the concept, and finally having them commit to it.

A second key commitment that we negotiated with the Canadian partners was a willingness to do whatever it takes to create a win/win/win solution with regard to ownership. Specifically, that meant a win for each of them individually, a win for the firm, and a win for any stakeholders (partners, clients, etc.). At first, some of the partners doubted that a solution could satisfy the triple-win formula. In response to this skepticism, we used a tool from Edward DeBono's "Six Thinking Hats" approach to problem solving. We asked each participant to put on what DeBono calls the "yellow hat," which directs the wearer to put a positive spin on any suggested solutions. (In contrast, black-hat wearers ask, "What's wrong with this idea?")[2] With their yellow hats on, these owners were encouraged to use their imaginations in a positive, "can do" way.

With these two powerful guiding principles in place—playing above the line and the yellow hat—the owners dove in and created three different scenarios for solving the ownership issue. In less than four hours, the nine of them brainstormed three new possibilities on an issue that had stymied them for the better part of two years. The key was clearing enough mental space to imagine new ideas. Watching them create a breakthrough on this problem was the strongest example we have yet seen to support the claim that *nothing constructive happens from below the line*. When an individual or a whole team goes below the line, the thinking shifts from open and creative to defensive and closed—from "Let's learn and explore" to "Let's show why we're right." For this reason, we recommend that teams become expert at spotting defensiveness, so that no time is spent trying to debate something from below the line. It's wasted effort.

REAL-TIME USE OF THE DEFENSIVENESS SCALE

One of the most powerful exercises that we do with senior investment teams is a live, 360-degree evaluation. We gather the senior team together, explain the principle of choosing curiosity over defensiveness, and then ask them if they'd like to give candid feedback to and receive it from the team. Usually team members experience both excitement and fear when given this invitation. (We have yet to get a blasé reaction, such as "Whatever . . . .")

The person receiving feedback is instructed to clear his or her mind and notice, during the delivery of the feedback, whether he or she remains open and receptive or becomes closed and defensive. Often, the person receiving feedback will say something like, "I'm open to that feedback." When asked, "How do you know you're open to it?," the person often responds, "Because I agree with it." (The reverse is true, too: "I am not open to it because the feedback is wrong.")

When we hear these sorts of responses, we coach the receiving person that being open to feedback and agreeing with it are two different things. Imagine an X axis with one continuum, open versus defensive, and a Y axis with another continuum, agree versus disagree. A person can be open and disagree. Likewise, she can be closed and agree. The real key in either case is whether the receivers of feedback want to know more about the feedback. Do they want to ask the provider additional questions so that they can more fully understand the feedback? Are they curious?

We recently worked with a CIO who received feedback that he wasn't making full use of the department's resources. When asked if he was open to hearing this, he said, "Oh, yes, and it's true."

We then asked, "Do you want to learn more about it?"

His response was, "No, because I know where he's coming from."

We probed a little bit more and asked, "If that's true, then can you elaborate on what he meant?" After some reflection, the CIO took a guess at what he thought the feedback provider was thinking. We asked the provider, "Is this accurate?"

His response was, "Partially, but not fully."

Turning back to the receiving CIO, we said, "So, do you want to know more fully what he meant?"

Rather sheepishly, the CIO admitted that he would like to learn more, and that he had been closed to learning more because he'd assumed that he knew what the other person thought.

This is often the case: Smart people assume that they know. Despite all the research into the phenomenon of overconfidence, smart people still fall into the trap. One important way to avoid overconfidence is to hone your skills at recognizing defensiveness. Being open to all feedback and new ideas is a sure way to avoid arrogance in thinking. Teams that sharpen their learning skills will thus gain a considerable edge in their ability to outperform slow-learning teams.

Our experience working with investment teams leads to two important conclusions:

1. Most smart people are not top-notch learners by nature.
2. With practice, they can become top-notch learners.

SUMMARY

The Center for Creative Leadership (CCL), hailed by *Business Week* magazine as the world's top think-tank on leadership training, has created a list of 67 attributes of leaders. Further, the CCL has studied these attributes as predictors of success and concluded that the number-one trait of top leaders is learning agility—the very behavior discussed in this chapter. Leaders and team members of top investment teams understand the three key steps of learning agility:

1. Recognize when you've become defensive.
2. Make a choice to shift back to being open and curious.
3. Develop several reliable shift-moves for getting back above the line when you've fallen below it.

To the degree that your investment team can master these skills, you will set yourselves apart from other teams. Remaining open and curious is the key.

NEXT STEPS

Now, as you finish this chapter, ask yourself:

- Did I get defensive about any of this material? Did I refute it in my head? Did I reread the credentials of the authors to dig up some shortcomings (that is, reasons why I can dismiss their arguments)?
- As you read about the other key behaviors, continue this exercise of monitoring your own defensiveness. And remember: It's natural

to get defensive. The real test of excellence is how quickly you notice it and change your behavior and thinking.

- What are some of the biggest "learnings" that you have had about investing? Did you resist these discoveries or get them quickly?
- What is the most recent learning that you have gotten? (If you can't think of a recent one, you're ripe for lots of great new learning if you employ the material from this chapter.)
- What is your most common pattern of defensiveness? When does it occur? What is one step you can take to recognize that pattern sooner and shift back to learning?
- How do you respond to defensiveness when you see it in your teammates? Do you escalate the behavior by getting defensive yourself?
- Can you find situations in your firm in which to use the Defensiveness Scale? (Examples: during a yearly performance review, or when a stock goes south and the team is doing the postmortem.)
- How can you change the tone of the meetings you lead or participate in to encourage people to drop their defenses?

CHAPTER 3

Accountability Part 1
Taking Responsibility

Jim Dethmer

Boss: The project post-mortem will only be helpful if each of us is honest about what went wrong.
Staff Member: Your colossal ineptitude as a leader suppressed our natural talents, leaving us listless and unfocused.
Boss: And by "honest" I mean blaming people who aren't here.
—Scott Adams, in a "Dilbert" cartoon

The newly appointed CEO of a small West Coast firm called us last summer to talk about the issues he was facing in his new role. "Jim," he said, "I'm really frustrated. We have lots of talent on this team, but something's just not clicking for us. We're not producing the performance I know we're capable of, and our clients are starting to question our investment process. I'm afraid the future does not look good—but it should." When we probed into the way the team members were working together, the number-one issue became quite clear: "It's accountability—it seems like no one is willing to step up and be accountable," the troubled CEO concluded. "That is our biggest challenge."

When firms contact the Focus Consulting Group to ask for help in becoming more effective, we ask them what particular issues they see as impediments to their effectiveness. Like our West Coast firm, one issue that surfaces with almost every firm is accountability. We regularly hear leaders say, "We need more accountability," or "No one around here is willing to step up and be accountable." In fact, in Focus Consulting's

"Values Survey" database, accountability comes in second only to team-work/collaboration as the highest-rated value when investment firm employees are asked to identify key values and behaviors they need to strengthen to be more successful.

Among investment firms, there are a number of common scenarios in which people are looking for accountability:

- When a stock underperforms expectations.
- When the information packet given to a prospective institutional mutual fund client contains mistakes.
- When a system upgrade is not delivered by the due date.
- When an incorrect accounting entry affects performance reporting.
- When a mid-cap value fund is underperforming.
- When the firm is not attracting the kind of talent it needs.

In these days of Sarbanes-Oxley and Eliot Spitzer, accountability is more than just a good idea or a "nice to have." It is often the life or death of an organization. We all know this—so why is accountability still such an issue in investment firms? Why do we have to legislate accountability? Perhaps a more important question is, "*Can* we legislate accountability?" Even as compliance departments grow larger and database checks and balances become more complex, accountability still cannot be guaranteed. A practical question that merits attention is, "Can small- and mid-sized mutual fund firms even afford to be accountable?" We know that they cannot afford *not* to be accountable, but can they pay the financial price required for accountability?

The Focus Consulting Group takes a very different approach to accountability. We understand the need for compliance departments, reporting requirements, database management, and attorneys general, but we think the accountability issue can never be finally and fully resolved until we *change our thinking about what accountability actually is*.

WHAT IS ACCOUNTABILITY?

Let's get back to basics. In concrete terms, the word *accountability* means "to account for what has been done." The focus of the word is in the past:

"to account for what has been done *in the past*." Its synonyms are *blame* and *fault*: "Whose fault is it?" "Who's to blame?" The context for accountability is usually that something has gone wrong. Rarely do we hear teams trying to figure out who's accountable for what went right. When was the last time your firm called an emergency meeting to determine who was accountable for assets under management growing by 10 percent over the last 6 months, or for outperforming the benchmark by 350 basis points?

We learned an interesting exercise in accountability from one of our mentors, Katie Hendricks, PhD. When working with an investment team, we ask the participants to pass around a crisp $100 bill. Naturally, their interest is immediately piqued. After everyone in the room has had a chance to touch and examine the bill, we tape it to a flip chart in the front of the room. With everyone staring in puzzlement, we begin our teaching on accountability by asking one simple question: "Who is responsible for that $100 bill being there?"

The first response is usually, "You are! You put it there."

This is the normal understanding of accountability. Usually we first try to answer the question, "Who did it?" The normal thinking is that because I "did it," I am responsible.

We listen to the responses and then ask again, "Who is responsible for that $100 bill being there?" The audience usually becomes a bit frustrated that the first answer wasn't accepted. Undaunted, they try again.

"We are! We all touched it."

This is also a common view of accountability. "Let's figure out who participated in the chain of events that led to the outcome. Whoever participated is responsible."

Have you ever been involved in one of these witch hunts? A deadline is missed and the team leader gathers everyone in the room to reconstruct the chain of events that led to the deadline being missed. With this approach to accountability, there is usually plenty of blame and fault to go around.

Without responding, we simply ask the question again, "Who is responsible for that $100 bill being there?"

Now those who take the root-cause approach to accountability often speak up:

"The U.S. government is. They made the bill."

"Trees are. They were the source of the paper."

"Adam and Eve. They made the first mistake."

This is the "who started it" approach to accountability. "The analyst is responsible because she's the one who first suggested that the stock was a good buy." "The receptionist is responsible. He routed the call to the wrong place in the beginning."

The common theme in all these answers, and in what we call the old view of accountability, is *blame* and *fault*. This view of accountability is determined by:

- Who did it?
- Who participated in it?
- Who started it?

In all of these cases, accountability is *assigned*. Usually an authority figure assigns accountability to someone—that is, to someone who is to blame.

As we go to press in the aftermath of Hurricane Katrina, I have found two articles in the *Chicago Tribune* that highlight this widespread phenomenon of assigning blame. In fact, the title of one article is "Why Do We Always Assign Blame?" In it the author noted, "Maybe the finger-pointing comes from today's mindset that someone else always must be ready and in charge of ensuring our safety and comfort."[1] Another columnist titled his article, "Disaster Leads to Premature Blame Game" and elaborated, "It took no time after New Orleans was flooded for commentators to start ladling out blame by the barrel."[2] Perhaps this tendency toward blaming is the reason a new word has appeared in the dictionary: *blamestorming*.

When firms contact us for help with accountability, it usually turns out that those in authority are asking how they can get people to accept blame and fault for the mistakes they have made. Can you see why this approach doesn't work? In reality, has it ever worked?

Did it work when your parents gathered you and your siblings together to figure out how the picture window in the family room got broken, or the new car got scratched, or the dog got lowered down the laundry chute?

Did it work when your coach tried to assign accountability for how a play was blown or the game was lost?

Does it work when you and your spouse try to figure out why your relationship isn't working and who's to blame?

Our answer, and our experience, is no. This approach simply does not work. (Unless of course, you are a contestant on Donald Trump's *The Apprentice* television show, where the proven strategy is to heap as much blame as possible on the other team members so that they get fired.)

By *work*, we mean that the issue gets resolved in a way that:

- Keeps an undesirable result from being repeated.
- Not only keeps relationships intact, but actually increases trust and productivity.
- Increases learning and growth for everyone involved.

At best, we believe the old view of accountability finds fault, assigns blame, and increases fear, guilt, and shame. All these outcomes leave toxic residue in the team or in the firm. (*The Apprentice* contestants largely agree that they never want to see each other again!) It is our belief and experience that this is the root cause of CYA[3] behavior.

So, what's a better, proven way that *does* work?

RADICAL RESPONSIBILITY

With the $100 bill still hanging on the flip chart, and with the frustration in the room growing, someone usually has a breakthrough thought. From the back of the room, someone stands and says, "I am! I am responsible for the $100 bill being there right now."

"Prove it," we say—but with genuine excitement, because we see a paradigm shifting before our very eyes.

With pride, the responsible one strides to the front of the room and takes the $100 bill off the flip chart. "I'm responsible because it's not there anymore!"

This is *radical responsibility*.

Old accountability looks to the past to assign fault and blame to those who did it, participated in it, or started it. Radical responsibility looks to the present and asks, "What can I learn from what has occurred?" or "What am I doing or not doing that is keeping this situation going?"

Just as *accountability* means "to account for what has been done in the past," so, too, *responsibility* means "to be able to respond"; that is, to be "response-able." Often teams are not able to respond to the present situation because they are too stuck in the past trying to figure out who did it or who's to blame.

A key difference between old accountability and radical responsibility is that old accountability is *assigned* and responsibility is *taken*. Old accountability is usually assigned by authority figures to the person whom they deem to be accountable for what has occurred. Many of us have heard an authority figure say, "I'm going to hold you accountable for making sure that it gets done."

Assigned accountability is not very effective. This is obvious if you look at the U.S. penal system. Jails are filled with people to whom accountability was assigned. In most cases, a judge or a jury operating on behalf of society has said, "You're accountable." However, a quick walk through a prison will tell you that this assignment of accountability has done these people (and society) little good. Most people in prison believe that they are innocent and victims of someone else: a buddy who ratted them out, a bad lawyer, a biased jury, a judge who didn't understand, or society in general.

Rarely does one come across prisoners who have taken responsibility for what has occurred in their lives. Until they do *take* responsibility (instead of having it thrust upon them), these persons will remain in the prison of blame and victimhood and miss out on all the learning that life has to offer.

RADICAL RESPONSIBILITY IN REAL LIFE

Fine; you're beginning to understand the base concept. Now, what does radical responsibility look like in the investment industry?

Consider this example involving the top four leaders of one of the preeminent investment firms in the United States, one respected for both its long-term performance and its culture. One afternoon, we were doing an exercise in "appreciative inquiry" in which these leaders were sharing historical experiences that illustrated how their values were alive in the organization. The value we were talking about was *precision*. We asked them to tell us stories about precision and how it showed up in the firm. As a group, they became quite energized as they told the story of a young staff person in the organization who had been very precise in his use of words while writing an article that would appear under the CEO's byline in a monthly financial magazine. (For some time, the firm had been issuing a monthly article, and the writing job had usually fallen to the president, who is a gifted writer and spokesperson for the company.)

As the story unfolded, it became clear that the CEO was learning about the content of that particular article for the first time. Someone mentioned that the magazine had asked that the article be about CEOs of organizations who had outstayed their effectiveness. The CEO of the investment firm asked the team whom they had chosen as an illustration of an outmoded CEO. When they named the person they had chosen, the CEO reacted with quick clarity, saying, "You can't write about him. He is a friend of mine and we serve together on the board of a company."

An awkward silence fell over the room. What had been, only a few seconds earlier, a celebration of a young staffer's commitment to precision had turned into an awkward moment of embarrassment. The CEO, in a matter-of-fact tone, demanded that another article be written about someone else.

The president turned a bad moment into a worse moment by saying, "We can't. The article has already gone to print and there is nothing we can do about it." A thick and heavy silence filled the room.

Our perspective was that of consultants who had been working with this team for more than a year on the behaviors of high-performing teams. We recognized that, although this was a most challenging situation, it was also a real-world opportunity for them to put what they had learned into action. You can imagine that this situation had the potential to turn ugly very fast. Under old-accountability thinking, two things would have happened. First, everyone would have pointed fingers at everyone else to simultaneously deflect and assign blame. Second, the hapless staffer would have been singled out not as an example of the company's commitment to precision, but as the poster child for incompetence.

None of these things happened.

The president spoke first and *took responsibility*. "It's my fault." Speaking to the CEO, he said, "I know everyone you relate to and work with and it is inexcusable that this slipped by me."

The CEO was next to step to the plate and, in turn, *take responsibility*. "No, it's my responsibility. I have had the sense for some time that we should stop writing a monthly article. It served us well at one time, but I think we have been stretched too thin and this article has become more of a burden than anything else. I should have spoken up and this kind of thing wouldn't have happened."

For the next few minutes, everyone in the room took turns *taking responsibility*. They also did a marvelous job of owning their feelings and modeling emotional intelligence, which we'll discuss in more detail in Chapter 7 (on awareness).

Once they had taken responsibility and processed their emotions, they snapped into action, immediately deciding what had to be done to make the best of a bad situation. Phone calls were made and letters sent. Relationships were rescued from sure disaster and process improvements were made to guarantee that nothing like this would ever happen again.

Quickly and effectively, these leadership team members absorbed all the learnings they could get from the situation. Without placing blame or assigning accountability, they had stepped into radical responsibility.

The ending of this story punctuates the point of radical responsibility. Several weeks later, at the close of the quarter, the president, who was tasked with proposing bonus allotments to the CEO and the board, chose to dock his own bonus because of his lapse in this situation. No one had to hold him accountable and make sure that he had learned his lesson. He guaranteed that he got the learnings and the lessons.

Too good to be true? Not from our perspective. We see this kind of radical responsibility regularly in firms that have a commitment to learning and effectiveness. Old accountability is too slow and leads to low learning because it induces blame, shame, guilt, and fear—states not conducive to optimal growth and learning. In the investment industry, we have seen that firms committed to a culture of optimal growth and learning are more creative and successful because of their engaged and highly productive employees. We have seen that this commitment is a key differentiating characteristic of long-term, highly successful investment firms.

The preceding story also illustrates another powerful principle of radical responsibility: *speed of the leader, speed of the team*. Notice that in the example, the leaders went first in taking responsibility. So often leaders look first to their teams to see who made the mistake or to find what went wrong. We believe that great leaders look first to *themselves*, to see how they created the existing situation by what they said or didn't say or by what they did or didn't do.

SLICING THE 100 PERCENT PIE

One perspective that has to change if you want to step into radical responsibility is the belief that for any given situation, there is 100 percent responsibility and the goal is to apportion that 100 percent accurately. We call this "slicing the pie." We've all done it. This is the "you're 70% responsible and I'm 30% responsible" (or 60/40, 80/20, 90/10) way of thinking.

In my marriage counseling days, I saw this on a regular basis. Couples would come to me with a problem and want me to slice the pie of responsibility. They had tried on their own to assign responsibility, but it only led to more fighting, so they ended up coming to someone they perceived as a professional pie-slicer to show them the way. If I accepted this invitation and bought into this way of thinking, it guaranteed that all three of us would get stuck in the quagmire of blame and criticism.

The way out for such couples was to see that there was not 100 percent responsibility but, rather, 200 percent responsibility. In all situations, there is enough responsibility for each person to take 100 percent responsibility . . . if they choose to take it.

Suppose for a moment that a couple's particular issue is their 13-year-old son's failing grades at school. Her version of the story is that the father is 90 percent to blame because he travels too much and isn't available to his son. His version of the story is that she is 80 percent to blame because she is too soft on their son and won't enforce discipline. In old-accountability thinking, each spouse is assigning blame to the other for what he or she is doing or not doing that is causing the problem. This mindset leads to blame and criticism and staying stuck.

The shift for such a couple occurs when they realize that they are each 100 percent responsible for creating the problematic situation. He could stop blaming her and start wondering about what he is doing in the marriage and family that causes them to have a rebellious 13-year-old.

Maybe it's because he travels three weeks out of every month. Or because he feels awkward talking to his son about anything except sports and cars. Or maybe it's because he himself was a rebellious 13-year-old who drove his parents crazy, and he has never resolved those issues. She, along the same lines, could wonder about how she has created a situation in which she is in a constant power struggle with her son. Maybe she doesn't know how to set limits and hold boundaries. Or maybe she is afraid to lose her son's love, which has become of utmost importance to her because she and her husband don't really relate much any more.

When each spouse takes 100 percent responsibility and starts getting curious about how they *each* created the situation about which they are complaining, they are on the road to radical responsibility—and a better marriage and family life.

This view of responsibility is not just some mathematical sleight of hand; relational "new math," if you will. It really is a different way of being in the world. The best situation one can hope for when operating with a pie-slicing mentality is that each person will take 50 percent responsibility. This view, however, requires that the other person be willing to take 50 percent responsibility in order for the problem to be solved. Under the radical-responsibility view of 200 percent responsibility, I can take my 100 percent regardless of what the other person does or does not do. I can get my learnings and my growth whether or not the other person gets his or hers. My life, my learnings, my fun, my joy, my success are not in any way dependent on the other person playing along. (There is a wonderful line in the movie *The Great Raid*, in which the commander of a Japanese prison says to an American prisoner, "If you will help me, I can arrange for your release." The POW shakes his head. Angrily, the commander says, "I am offering you an opportunity to have a future!" The POW then delivers an incredibly powerful response: "My future is not in your hands.")

Furthermore, we have noticed that if one person in a situation is willing to take 100 percent responsibility and stop blaming herself or others, it often has the effect of ending blame and criticism for everyone. One person can change the entire game. The goal is pictured in Figure 3.1.

The goal is to take 100 percent responsibility: no less, no more. When we take less than 100 percent responsibility, we are in "victim" space, or "at the effect of" what someone else is doing or not doing. When we take more than 100 percent responsibility, we often end up in "hero"

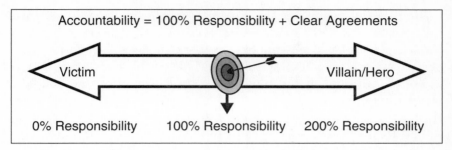

Accountability = 100% Responsibility + Clear Agreements

Victim   Villain/Hero

0% Responsibility   100% Responsibility   200% Responsibility

FIGURE 3.1   Arrow of 100% responsibility.

space. Taking either less or more than 100 percent is a mistake. If we take less than 100 percent responsibility, we end up blaming and complaining. If we take more than 100 percent responsibility, we end up rescuing and resenting. Neither party learns from the experience, for use in adapting for future situations, so the undesirable cycle repeats itself again and again.

We've all seen a situation in which one or more members of the team aren't carrying their weight; that is, they are taking less than 100 percent responsibility. When this occurs, someone else on the team usually steps up and rescues the "slackers" and the situation by taking more than 100 percent responsibility. This often looks like doing more than the hero's fair share, such as working longer hours or distorting the work/life balance. The hero does it for a while (rescuing), but we've learned that it's just a matter of time until the other shoe drops and the hero ends up resenting.

Unfortunately, many firms reward people for hero behavior. This is unfortunate because no team is optimally effective when some of its members are underfunctioning and others are overfunctioning. The best teams have everyone taking 100 percent responsibility. No more, no less.

BLAMING VERSUS CLAIMING

Another major difference between old accountability and new, radical responsibility is the difference between *blaming* and *claiming*. When teams operate under old accountability, a lot of blaming goes on. People blame each other and they blame themselves. Blame is toxic and leads to fear and shame. Most importantly, there is an inverse relationship between blame and learning. They cannot coexist—it is one or the other.

We want to make it clear that we include self-blame as toxic when it comes to learning. Often when we work with teams, we hear members saying things like:

- "It's my fault."
- "I screwed up."
- "I dropped the ball."
- "My bad."

Though we understand the sentiment behind such self-blame, we think it leads to low learning levels. When we experience blame, shame, guilt, and fear, we constrict. We pull back. We hide from ourselves, each other, and the situation. In contrast, claiming responsibility, being curious, living in wonder, and opening to learning expand us and make us open to the situation and all that we can learn from it.

The issue here is not so much the words we say as the attitude we have. We see high-performing teams claiming responsibility without adding constricting attitudes like shame, guilt, and fear. Believe it or not, in high-performing teams there is more of an attitude of playfulness around learning than an attitude of grim seriousness ("This is life or death"). Specialists in learning have known for years that people learn best when they are having fun, not when they are afraid. Just visit top-performing firms like Brandes, William Blair, or K.G. Redding and you will see people enjoying themselves.

This is why we advocate claiming responsibility while staying in a state of openness and fun, rather than constricting in blame. Here are some examples of two different ways of being in the workplace:

Blaming	Claiming
You're not listening to me.	I'm not communicating in a way that inspires listening or learning.
You don't get it.	I'm not effectively communicating what I'm saying.

Blaming	Claiming
You don't do what you say you're going to do.	I want to find out how we can keep our agreements with one another.
Why don't you stop micromanaging and let me do my job?	How can I build my credibility with you?
My bonus is out of my control.	What else can I do to contribute to the overall performance of the firm?
They've given me a bad benchmark to manage against.	How can I effectively demonstrate why this alternative benchmark is better?

Whenever we're blaming, we are pointing a finger at someone else or ourselves. When we are claiming, we are in a state of curiosity, wondering about how we are contributing to what is occurring.

THE RULE OF THREE

Gay Hendricks taught us the principle of the Rule of Three. The Rule of Three says that if something happens three or more times, take responsibility for it. In other words, if something undesirable happens in your life once or twice, consider it an accident or random happenstance. If something occurs three or more times, take responsibility for it and get the learnings.

- If someone takes credit for one of your ideas once or twice, ignore it. If they do it three times, take responsibility and ask yourself how you are creating this situation.
- If your boss is rude to you once or twice, chalk it up to a bad day on his or her part. If he or she is rude three times, get curious about how your relating with him or her is creating this situation. Have you trained this boss to be rude to you?
- If you get a cold once a year, consider it the law of nature. If you get three or more colds a year, take responsibility for your colds and get the learning. Research shows that people often get sick because

they don't want to face something that's going on at work. We
think there is a healthier way to deal with things you don't want
to face than to continue to literally make yourself sick.

This is radical responsibility and it leads to big learning and real growth.
When teams live this way, it is a winning formula.

COMMITTING TO RADICAL RESPONSIBILITY

If you want to give this new way of living a try, we recommend the following. First, make a personal commitment to radical responsibility. Try
saying something like this out loud to your self and notice what happens:

> "I commit to take responsibility for whatever is occurring in my life
> rather than blaming myself or anyone else."
> "I commit to be curious and to get all the learnings out of every
> situation."

When you say this out loud and really commit to what you're saying,
notice what happens. Does your mind introduce *"yes, buts"*?

- *Yes, but* if I do that, people will take advantage of me.
- *Yes, but* if I do that, I'll be the only one in the department doing
  it.
- *Yes, but* I don't know how to do this.
- *Yes, but* I'm afraid.

We believe in honoring our "yes, buts." We honor them by noticing
them and accepting them. They are indicators of some important resistance we have against going to the next level of effectiveness. One way of
honoring them is to say them out loud or write them down. Once you
write them down, ask yourself a few questions:

- Is this "yes, but" a **belief**? Is this belief axiomatically true and unarguable, like the law of gravity? Would I be willing to test this belief
  and replace it with one that more accurately conforms to reality?
  Chris Argyris of Harvard, mentioned earlier, uses the term *test* fre-

quently. We worked with a CIO who was certain that her boss would never agree to a solution we were proposing. We invoked the testing principle: Are you willing to test this perception? She was, and to her surprise the boss offered no resistance whatsoever to the idea. The obstacle had all been in her head.

We have learned over the years that many highly intelligent people have some really wrong beliefs: beliefs they learned from someone else a long time ago; beliefs they have never tested. For example, "If I take responsibility, people will take advantage of me" is a belief. It is not a rule of the universe. Would you be willing to test that belief?

- Is this "yes, but" a **fact**?

    For example, it might be a fact that you don't know how to take responsibility. Our question, though, is this: "Would you be willing to commit to taking responsibility and learn how after you commit?" Much of life works this way. How many of us knew how to be parents before we committed to being parents? How many of us knew how to drive before we committed to driving? Of course we don't know how. That's why it's called *learning*. But if we wait to commit until we know how, we often never commit. We've seen a lot of people who say, "I don't know how to have a relationship, so I'll just hold off committing."

- Is this "yes, but" a **feeling**?

    Almost always, when we make a new commitment, we have a feeling. Often that feeling is fear. Sometimes it's excitement. Sometimes it's both. We've learned that the best thing to do with feelings is to simply feel them, feel them right through to completion. Often this takes only about three or four breaths, until the feeling has dissipated. With feelings, we can either dissipate or constipate. *Constipating* feelings means getting them stuck—and stuck feelings produce all kinds of problems.

A great way to get clear about commitments is to try saying the counter-commitment and see if that feels real and honest. Go back and forth between the two commitments until one of them clicks for you and you know it is your clear intention. With radical responsibility, try these two commitments:

Radical Responsibility

"I commit to take responsibility for whatever is occurring in my life rather than blaming myself or anyone else."

Old Accountability

"I commit to blaming myself and others by finding fault and assigning blame."

STEPPING INTO COMMITMENT

Once you get a commitment to radical responsibility that sounds and feels real, try testing it in a real-life situation. Write down a situation from work in which you would normally either blame yourself or someone else:

Situation:_____

Now, from a stance of claiming responsibility, ask these questions. The goal is to ask the questions with an attitude of genuine curiosity and openness.

- How have I created this situation by what I have done or not done?
- How am I keeping this situation going?
- How is this situation familiar?
- What has this situation taught me that I couldn't have learned any other way?
- What is my subconscious payoff in keeping this situation going?
- From the past, this situation reminds me of . . . .

If you want to play the radical responsibility game as a team at work, try using this post-mortem process the next time something goes wrong. First, get clear as a team about your commitment to taking responsibility. Is every team member willing to take responsibility without blaming himself, herself, or anyone else (including people who are not on the team or not in the room)?

If the answer is yes, ask yourselves these questions out of genuine curiosity, not for the purpose of finding fault or placing blame.

- What happened? What are the facts? What actually occurred? (Consult Chapter 5 on candor so you can differentiate facts from stories.)
- With the facts on the table, play the "I Take Responsibility" game. Have all team members think up as many things as they can about how what they did or didn't do led to the situation. Share your thoughts in a round-robin fashion, with the team leader going first.
- What are the key learnings you can take from the situation?
- Did a process issue lead to the situation? If so, what is it?
- What changes can you (as a team) make in your processes to implement your learnings?
- How will you test to see if the process changes are effective?

Jim Collins says, "When you conduct autopsies without blame, you go a long way toward creating a climate where the truth is heard."[4] We couldn't agree more!

WHAT IF EVERYONE ISN'T PLAYING?

A question that often comes up when Focus Consulting is working with firms is: "What if I commit to radical responsibility and no one else on my team does?" Or more specifically, "What if I do and my boss doesn't?"

One investment firm we're familiar with had a department that hired a new executive assistant. It immediately became apparent that the assistant had significantly exaggerated his prior experience and skills, and eventually he was terminated. When the four-member team that had led the interviewing process debriefed on the situation, one team member stepped up and said, "If we'd had an Excel competency test for candidates, it would have been obvious [that the assistant wasn't capable]. I'm going to develop a test based on our needs and have HR sign off on it so we can use it for all future candidates." Each of the other three team members, instead of pointing out what they had learned from the experience and how they would adapt to improve the process, took a turn explaining why he or she had never *really* wanted to hire the assistant and how it *really* was the first person's fault in the end. What was the result?

- The first manager never exposed himself that way again.
- He no longer trusted the other members of the interview team.
- During future interview processes, he insisted on debriefing via e-mail so that he could document his position on each candidate.

Obviously, the team lost in many ways:

- Future good ideas like the Excel test were never mentioned, for fear that doing so would expose the suggester by making him or her look wrong.
- Productivity and efficiency were significantly reduced by the e-mail-only debriefings.
- Trust was significantly reduced, thus minimizing the team's capacity to take smart risks and be creative.

Obviously, high-performing teams can exist only when everyone has shared commitments. Our approach to working with teams is to help them get extremely clear about their commitments. This process usually involves some intense discussion about what they want and don't want. When a whole team commits to taking responsibility, great things can and do occur.

But what if your team or your boss (or your spouse or partner) doesn't want to live this way? What do you do then? Radical responsibility would invite you to take responsibility for the reality that you have a boss or partner who doesn't want to take responsibility, but would rather choose to blame and criticize. Go back to the earlier exercise and ask yourself all the questions associated with taking responsibility, starting with "How have I created this situation by what I have done or not done?" Walking through these questions often leads to a learning breakthrough.

If you are in such a situation, we think you have the following choices:

- Go along with the team or your boss and live with blame, criticism, and CYA behavior. This is a reasonable choice as a short-term safe play. In the longer term, however, we think it will be destructive to your career and your life. These are high stakes, and we have seen repeatedly that people who choose to live in blame, criticism, and fear for the long term experience all kinds of adverse effects in their lives.

- Live a radically different life and see what happens. Often people think they know what would happen if they lived the way we talk about living. They are certain that they would be taken advantage of, or laughed at, or dismissed outright. Our experience has shown, though, that what people are often sure is going to happen, doesn't actually happen. Life is far more complicated and mysterious than what we perceive or predict. If you are open to possibilities that you can't currently see because of your finite perspective, new outcomes often appear. Your beliefs about what will certainly happen if you live this way are often just an excuse to allow you to continue to take less than 100 percent responsibility and stay a victim. We have seen many examples of one person changing an entire situation by his willingness to take responsibility.

- Change jobs. We have seen people who understand what we're talking about come to the conclusion that life is too short to play on a team that is committed to blame and criticism and a fearful life. They "fire" their boss or their firm and open themselves up to the possibility of joining a new team that plays by new rules. This choice often brings some great questions into our lives, such as:
  - What am I willing to put at risk for my career satisfaction (for example, my current job, my status, my paycheck, my golden handcuffs)?
  - What do I value more than my happiness (for example, status quo, security, being liked)?
  - What am I willing to put at risk to live the life I want to live?

These are important and profound questions that often come up when we are coaching people. One way to understand these questions is to get clear about your commitments and pay attention to how your commitments differ from your boss's commitments or your firm's commitments.

CONCLUSION

Of all the behaviors we teach investment teams, this one of taking radical responsibility may be the most difficult to grasp. We think this difficulty springs from the fact that we live in a culture where blaming, being "at the effect of," and being a victim are the near-universal mindset. When anyone steps out of this way of being, they are truly on the road less traveled.

So why take the risk?

Many of you reading this book have built successful, financially lucrative careers within an environment of old accountability. You may be asking yourself why you should consider changing. The answer is simple: because of the results. The Focus Consulting Group works closely with many different firms in the investment industry, and we see firms that choose to adopt a culture of radical responsibility achieving the following results:

- They are more *nimble*, because they don't spend time looking for someone to punish. Employees are committed to learning instead of blaming. They demonstrate their learning agility by quickly extracting the lessons from their experiences, adapting their processes, and moving on to greater challenges.
- They are more *creative*, because people are encouraged and not afraid to take risks.
- They are *employers of choice*, because the accountable culture they've created is a breath of fresh air to employees. As a result, their voluntary turnover is lower than average.
- They make *fewer missteps when hiring*, because they know that accountability is one of their differentiating values. When they consider candidates, they focus on hiring for cultural fit and interview accordingly, rather than just hoping that a person with the right skills will fit in.

Can you imagine being part of a team or organization like this? Is that worth the risk? We think you will agree wholeheartedly that it is.

SUMMARY

- The old view of accountability finds fault, assigns blame, and increases fear, guilt, and shame.
- The new view of accountability = 100% responsibility + clear agreements.
- Accountability must be taken, not assigned.
- Every person must take exactly 100 percent responsibility—no more, no less.
- Organizations that embrace and practice true accountability throughout the entire organization are more nimble, are more creative, and have more empowered and fulfilled employees.

NEXT STEPS

- Decide if you are ready to commit to this definition of *accountability*. If so, make a personal commitment to being accountable. Claim, don't blame.
- Personally do the "Stepping into Commitment" exercise for an incident that recently took place.
- Introduce your team to this definition of *accountability*. Is everyone willing to commit to operating as part of this type of accountable team? If they seem willing to commit, get a clear yes from each team member.
- Introduce the team version of the "Stepping into Commitment" exercise to your team for an incident that recently took place. Remember, everyone should be asking "I" questions to take his or her own 100 percent responsibility.
- The very next time a situation occurs in which you find yourself blaming someone else for something, stop and ask yourself these questions:
    - How did I contribute to this situation?
    - What could I have done differently to avoid this outcome?
    - What did I learn from this experience?
    - How will what I learned change what I do in the future?

CHAPTER 4

Accountability Part 2
Making and Keeping Agreements

Jim Dethmer

There is no such thing as a small breach of integrity.
—Tom Peters

T he following scenario illustrates the second major challenge related to accountability. It's one that many investment firms deal with regularly.

It's 9:00 on Tuesday morning, time for the investment committee's weekly meeting. Two junior analysts are present along with a portfolio manager. During the next 20 minutes, the rest of the team wanders in, some offering brief apologies for being late, others simply taking their seats. Finally, at 9:25 AM, the CIO enters the room, explaining that he's late because of a conference call with a client that ran long. The meeting starts at 9:30 AM.

The second item on the "agenda" (*agenda* is in quotes here because there is no actual agenda, just a loose idea about what the team is there to do that day) is a presentation by the service-sector analyst on her findings related to ServiceMaster's Terminix business. She makes a solid case, but fails to address three concerns that the CIO says he raised in last week's meeting. The analyst says she doesn't remember him asking her to focus her research on those concerns, but recalls him saying that he wanted information on the implications of the drought in Florida on the termite business. They debate for 10 minutes about who said what. Others chime in with their recollections about what happened last week. Finally, they decide to postpone a decision on the stock until next week's meeting.

Internally, the analyst feels that the CIO has been unfair and hasn't treated her with respect. She also believes that he regularly loses track of what he has or hasn't said in meetings. She complains about it to a group of analysts at lunch that day. The CIO later talks to one of the portfolio managers about the analyst, raising concerns about her competency.

Back in the weekly meeting, the next order of business is to talk about the agenda for a meeting, scheduled for the next day, with the leaders of a company whose stock the investment firm owns. However, several people don't have the meeting on their calendars, and a few have it scheduled for conflicting times. A debate ensues about who knew what about the meeting and when they knew it. Finally, 20 minutes later, things are settled and the meeting moves on.

During the last 10 minutes of the meeting, the CIO tells the team that he wants them to spend less time watching CNBC. He's concerned that because this firm is a value shop, CNBC is just "noise" that distracts them from what is really important: the long-term perspective. People nod their heads but don't say what they really think for fear of getting into a big debate, or worse yet, getting "bitten" by the boss, whose fuse is now running short. They intend to keep doing what they have been doing but to be more careful about getting caught doing it.

The meeting adjourns 45 minutes after the appointed end time and everyone is late to their next meetings. The cycle continues throughout the day.

Sound familiar? Like a chapter from a *Dilbert* cartoon book entitled, "Death by Meetings."

One of the first things we at Focus Consulting do when we work with a firm is to attend some of its meetings as silent observers, just to see what is happening. We learn a lot about the culture of a company by observing meetings, which are a microcosm of the entire organization. The preceding example captures what we see on a regular basis.

"So," you might say, "what's the issue? Isn't this the way all companies work?"

Our answer is "No!" High-performing teams operate on an altogether different level.

WHAT'S THE ISSUE?

From our perspective, the issue illustrated in the opening story is the issue of accountability. More specifically, it is one critical aspect of accountability that we call *impeccable agreements*. In a nutshell, we see that investment firms do best when they are completely scrupulous—impeccable—about making and keeping agreements. Accountability is not a problem in firms when people take 100 percent responsibility and are impeccable in their behavior concerning agreements. Our formula is this:

Accountability = 100% responsibility
                    + impeccable agreements

Before we go any further, we'd like you to stop for a minute and take the following Impeccable Agreements Self-Assessment Quiz. Taking it will orient you to what we are talking about in this chapter. Simply check the boxes that are true about you.

- ☐ I know that keeping agreements increases personal energy, rather than seeing agreements as others making me do something.
- ☐ I know how to consistently make clear agreements with others.
- ☐ I know how to select agreements that I do want to make.
- ☐ I know how to see when an agreement is necessary and how to proactively create agreements that I want to make.
- ☐ I know how to make agreements that are important to me; I can feel my body/emotions in concert with them.
- ☐ I do *not* make agreements that I don't want to make; I notice feelings/tension in my body when presented with agreements I don't want to sign up to.

☐ I enter into agreements initiated by others clearly and consciously.
☐ I keep the agreements I make.
☐ I can be counted on to do what I say I will do.
☐ I can be counted on *not* to do what I say I will not do.
☐ I know how to handle instances when I break agreements.
☐ I know how to handle instances when others break agreements with me.
☐ I know how to change agreements that are not working.
☐ Others keep their agreements with me, and if they don't, I know how to take 100 percent responsibility for creating and clearing up the situation.
☐ I am able to clearly formulate agreements and keep track of them. (Out of mind and on paper/in Outlook frees up my creative energy.)

How did you do? Our experience is that most people have holes in their lives when it comes to making and keeping agreements impeccably. In fact, our associates at Worth Ethic Corporation, Kate Ludeman and Eddie Erlandson, estimate that only about 3 percent of all people are impeccable concerning agreements. This reality leads to major accountability gaps. Before you decide that we're too picky or too pessimistic, let us explain what we mean by *agreements* and *impeccability*.

WHAT IS AN AGREEMENT?

Simply put, an *agreement* is anything I have said I will do or anything I have said I will not do. The following are examples of agreements.

- We won't use soft dollars under any circumstances.
- We won't allow market timing by any clients.
- I'll have the report on your desk by Monday morning at 10:00.
- I'll give John a call by noon and confirm his availability for the meeting.
- I won't talk to anyone about what we discussed in this conversation.
- We'll meet you for dinner at 6:00 on Tuesday at Curly's Pub.

- I'll pick up a gallon of milk on my way home from work.
- I will be home by 8:00.

Another important thing to note about agreements is that they are between two or more people. This is in contrast to *commitments*, which are between you and yourself, or you and the universe, or you and a Higher Power. Much of Focus Consulting's work with companies is built around helping people get clear and conscious about their commitments. For example, what is your commitment about feedback? We suggest a commitment like this, "I commit to being curious rather than defensive in the face of feedback." Notice that this commitment is not an agreement. Rather, it is a statement of how you intend to have your energy organized in life.

Can you see how this commitment is different from the agreements in the preceding list? An agreement simply says what I will do or won't do. Agreements exist between two or more people and are specific regarding *who* is going to do *what* by *when*. Commitments, in contrast, are more general, stating the intended direction of one's life.

In summary, an *agreement* is:

- Anything you have said you will or won't do.
- Between you and another person.
- Clear about who will do what by when.

MAKING GOOD AGREEMENTS

The key to being impeccable about agreements is learning how to make solid agreements in the first place. The most common problem we see with broken agreements is that people made poor agreements in the first place. There are three steps to making good agreements:

1. Only make agreements that you really want to make and that you feel fully aligned with when you make them.
2. Only make agreements about things over which you have control.
3. Record your agreements.

Only Make Agreements That You Really Want to Make and That You Feel Fully Aligned with When You Make Them

The most common problem we see involving agreements is that people enter into agreements that they didn't want to make in the first place, or about which they withheld significant facts or feelings. In these situations, a sloppy agreement is made, and sloppy agreements almost always get broken or completed in a shoddy way.

We see this all the time on teams that are not performing at their best. It often looks and sounds like this:

Scenario 1

Bill says, "Jerry, will you cover for me next week at the dinner with the marketing department? My son has a basketball game I really want to see."

Jerry responds without thinking, checking his calendar, or checking in with himself to see if this is something he really wants to do. "Sure," he says, without making eye contact.

Next Tuesday comes around and one of the following happens:

- Jerry forgets about the meeting and doesn't remember it until he sees Bill on Wednesday, at which point he panics and starts thinking up an excuse.
- Jerry shows up 40 minutes late for the meeting. He hates being there, doesn't make any valid contribution, and spends the time wishing he had never said yes to Bill.
- Jerry gets sick and can't attend the meeting.

Scenario 2

Joan, the portfolio manager, says, "Sarah, I need you to rewrite your presentation on XYZ Corporation."

Sarah, the analyst, nods. This is the *corporate nod*, which is actually intended to say one of the following:

- That's a stupid idea but you're the boss and you control my bonus.

- If I nod, I can end this conversation, and at least 50 percent of the time you'll forget that you asked me to do this in the first place.
- Whatever!

Each of these common occurrences is an illustration of entering into an agreement carelessly or callously, as opposed to entering into agreements consciously. High performers realize that making an agreement they didn't want to make in the first place is a surefire way to waste lots of energy that could be better invested in individual and team effectiveness.

We encourage people to ask themselves the following two questions before they enter into agreements:

1. Do I *want* to make that agreement?
2. Do I *really* want to make that agreement?

We coach people that unless your answer to both is a clear yes, don't make the agreement. By a *clear yes*, we mean a fully-in-the-game, no-holding-back, no-second-guessing, both-feet-fully-in-the-water affirmative. Sometimes we call it a "full-body yes," meaning that every part of and place in your body is aligned with the yes; there is no resistance anywhere in your body. (See Chapter 7 on awareness for tips on tuning into what your body is telling you.)

> *Exercise*: For the next week, when someone asks you do something (enter into an agreement), whether it is big (change jobs) or small (pick up a gallon of milk), ask yourself the two "want to" questions and check for a full-body yes:
>
> 1. Do I *want* to make that agreement?
> 2. Do I *really* want to make that agreement?

For now, go ahead and enter into whatever agreements you want just as you would have in the past. As the week goes on, notice what happens with agreements for which you had a clear yes and what happens with agreements for which you had anything other than a clear yes. Our experience shows that the agreements for which you had a clear yes will get done effortlessly and effectively, with little attendant drama. Agreements that you made without a clear yes might get done, but you will expend great effort to meet those commitments and you won't get much enjoyment from doing them. It's also a good possibility that you won't do them at all and that the situation revolving around this agreement will degenerate into drama. Because you are an investment professional who thrives on gathering information, we encourage you to keep a record of what happens so that you will have the data. After all, data is important to you for making decisions.

At this point, when we are giving a speech or facilitating an offsite, someone will raise a hand and say, "Are you suggesting that we only do what we want to do?" Our answer is, "Only if you want to be optimally effective." If you want to live with a lot of unnecessary stress and drama, and never make your genius contribution to the world (see Chapter 8 on genius), go ahead and make a lot of agreements you don't really want to make in the first place. The commenter then often brings up the problem of authority, and queries whether people are supposed to ask the two "want to" questions when their bosses ask them to do something.

There is a difference between agreements and edicts or orders. For years, we have taught leaders that they will be more effective if they learn the difference between agreements and edicts. There is a place for both in the investment world, but we've seen that the skillful leaders know when to use each technique.

An *agreement* is bilateral; both parties are fully in the game from the outset. An *edict* is unilateral; I am the boss, I want you to do this, and I don't care whether you want to do it or what you think about it. Just do it! Agreements tend to engender high buy-in, but take more time to structure effectively. Edicts often have low buy-in but can be delivered quickly. Generally, we suggest using edicts when you have a tight time frame and/or the issue does not require much buy-in or ownership on the part of others. We suggest using the Clarity Worksheet (found later in this chapter) when buy-in and ownership are important, when you are open to feedback from subordinates, and when you are not under serious time pressure.

Only Make Agreements about Things over Which You Have Control

One common mistake we see concerning agreements is that people make agreements about things they don't control. This usually leads to frustration and broken agreements. One coaching practice we regularly take people through is asking them to sort their work life into two buckets: (1) things they can control, and (2) things they can't control. We've found that most people do better when they separate these two buckets and when they devote their attention and energy to things they can control. A few simple illustrations will demonstrate the point:

- You can't control whether it rains. You can control whether or not you carry an umbrella.
- You can't control how your manager treats you. You can control how you respond to how she treats you.
- You (generally) can't control whether the bond you purchased is downgraded to junk status. You can control the analysis and decision-making process you used to determine whether you should purchase and continue to hold the bond.

Exercise: Take out a piece of paper and make two columns. Label one column "I Can Control" and label the other column "I Can't Control." Now take each of the items in the following list and put them in one of the two columns:

- How hard your teammates work.
- The investment process you use.
- Whether someone keeps his or her agreements with you.
- The securities contained in your discretionary portfolio.
- The total return of your discretionary portfolio.
- How much you make in a given year.
- Who you work for at your current company.
- How many hours you work.
- Whether you keep your agreements.

- What you get on a performance review, the form for which is actually completed by someone else (not to be confused with your actual performance, which is under your control).
- How much you'll sell to institutional investors (not to be confused with how much effort you put into selling to institutional investors, which you control. The buying decision is theirs and out of your control.)
- How your clients feel about you.
- Whether your firm is bought out.
- How long your daily commute to work takes.

Often when we give people this exercise, they want to introduce a third column, "Things I can influence." In our view, the introduction of this column would confuse the process and bring less clarity to agreements. It's important to place our full attention on things we can control. For items you feel belong in a "Things I can influence" column, you can choose to break them down into their components and then categorize the components as in your control or not in your control. For instance, what you get on your performance review breaks down to:

- Did I achieve the goals we established at the beginning of the year?
- Did I complete the development courses I committed to doing?
- Did I choose to perform my job in alignment with the values of the firm?
- Did I make time to meet with my manager during the year to gauge her assessment of my performance?
- How will my manager rate my performance on a scale of 1 to 10?

Going back to the list in the exercise, our experience shows that it should be sorted as in Table 4.1. Our observation is that effective, fulfilled people clearly differentiate between the things they can control and the things they can't control. They focus their time and energy on the things they can control. When it comes to making agreements, they only make agreements about things they can control.

What often happens is that someone will want you to make an agreement about something you can't control or that is actually under the control of someone else. For example, you're asked to make an agreement

TABLE 4.1   Control/Can't Control Differentiation

Things You CAN Control	Things You CAN'T Control
The investment process you use	How hard your teammates work
The securities contained in your discretionary portfolio	The total return of your discretionary portfolio
How many hours you work	Whether or not someone keeps his or her agreements with you
Whether you keep your agreements	Who you work for at your current company
How long your daily commute to work takes	How your clients feel about you
How much you make in a given year	Whether your firm is bought out
	What you get on your performance review
	How much you sell to institutional investors

about delivering numbers to the board at the April board meeting. The resources needed to gather the numbers are under the control of another department. Before you make the agreement to present the numbers at the board meeting, we suggest that you first get an agreement from the department head who controls the number-gathering.

"Ahhhh," you say. "This sounds complicated. Do you mean that for every agreement I make where I don't control all the factors, I should go to those who do control the factors and make agreements with them before I make an agreement with people who are depending on me?" Our answer is yes. Remember, our findings are that a commitment to being impeccable concerning agreements will actually make you more effective and reduce stress in your life. Deciding to live impeccably around agreements will organize your priorities and change the way you show up in life.

A commitment to live impeccably around agreements works best if it is a firm-wide or team-wide commitment with which everyone gets on board. This creates a context for someone saying to the boss, "I don't control that information or that resource. I'll try to get an agreement with those who do and get back to you with a clear agreement."

When we start teaching this material in a firm, we usually start with the executive team. After they have committed to living this way, they start to implement the behaviors. Once implemented, it is essential to teach the rest of the firm so that each person can make a conscious choice about his or her commitments and intentions. Once there is a common commitment about making and keeping agreements, everyone is speaking the same language and things flow much more smoothly.

Recently, we were leading a training for all the vice presidents and directors who reported to a firm's executive team. The executive team members had been through the training and they were beginning to use impeccable agreement practices. As you might expect, their direct-reporting staff had experienced a seismic change in the way things were being done. They were confused and a little frustrated. Once they understood the new way of making and keeping agreements, though, they "got it" and settled down. One thing they were quick to point out to the executive team was that the executives were using agreement language while still issuing edicts. We brought both groups together and taught them the simple practice of asking, "Is this an agreement or an edict?" When faced with this question, the executives began to pause and make conscious choices about what they thought was best for the firm.

Record Your Agreements

The third key to making great agreements is to write down your agreements. Our mentor Gay Hendricks has said that if your life is any more complicated than that of a Bedouin sheep herder, you need to write down your agreements. We agree and have experienced first hand the benefits of capturing all our agreements.

The biggest benefit to writing down your agreements—along with your appointments, projects, and tasks—is that it frees your mind up to be present in the current experience. We've learned for ourselves that unless we write down agreements, a portion of our minds will be used to remember what we said we would get done by Tuesday at 5:00. This portion of the mind is sometimes conscious, but more often it is unconscious. Like an iceberg, much of the mind is "below the surface," and we store agreements below the surface when we make them. This is what leads to the experience of waking up at 3:00 AM panicked by the thought that you promised to get your boss something but you can't remember exactly what it was or when you said you'd get it done. This is also why, in the middle of an important conversation, your mind will suddenly start to nag you about something it wants to make sure you remember. (Albert Einstein, one of the greatest minds of the 20th century, did not commit his telephone number to memory. His philosophy was, "Why should I clutter my brain with that when I can easily look it up?")

If you write down your agreements, and your mind can trust that you'll revisit what you have written down on a timely basis and complete it, then your mind will relax and be completely available to the present moment. A key skill of world-class leaders is their ability to be completely present and focused on whatever is before them right now, whether it is this present conversation, e-mail, phone call, article, or book. (We think this ability to focus is so important that we named our company after it!) These leaders don't waste time having to revisit things over and over again because they were only partially present when they encountered it the first time. One of the things that keeps people from being present and focused is that they haven't kept an accurate record of their agreements.

It doesn't matter whether you keep a yellow legal pad filled with everything you need to do or whether you store it all on your Blackberry and hotsync with Outlook. As long as your system works for you, it works. Here we define *works* by looking at whether anything slips through the cracks and whether or not you are able to focus, to be present and undistracted in the moment.

If this is an area of weakness that you haven't been able to improve on your own, we have two suggestions. First, read David Allen's book, *Getting Things Done*,[1] a succinct and practical book about getting organized and being more efficient. Alternatively, or in addition, you can hire a personal productivity coach, who will help you set up an organization system that works for you.

To review, the first step in becoming impeccable about keeping agreements, and therefore living an accountable life, is to make good agreements. The keys to making good agreements are to make agreements you want to make, to make agreements about things you have control over, and to write your agreements down. The next step on the road to impeccability is to keep your agreements.

KEEP YOUR AGREEMENTS

Tom Peters once said that there is no such thing as a small breach of integrity.[2] We agree. We also think that there is no such thing as a small broken agreement. If you want to have the highest-performing culture possible, and if you want to maximize energy and productivity, keep all your agreements. Broken agreements sap energy and create a culture of excuses, explanations, denial, and deceit. These are toxic elements and, like barnacles on the bottom of a boat, will keep you from running at maximum speed and efficiency.

Though it seems obvious that some agreements are weightier than others (for example, "I agree to be faithful to my wife" versus "I agree to pick up a gallon of milk on the way home from work"), at some level our minds can't tell the difference. To our minds, there is simply an open circuit that must be closed. Though we might feel greater guilt and anxiety about failing to keep some agreements over others, and though there might be greater relational and professional consequences to breaking some agreements over others, at the energetic level our minds simply read them all as open circuits that have to be completed.

The Focus Consulting Group has worked with executives who have dozens of open circuits, ranging from being constantly late to appointments, to never writing the letter of recommendation they promised a former employee, to failing to honor the bonus structure they promised their department, to breaking laws they had agreed to keep. We find, without exception, that when they commit to keeping *all* their agreements, their lives work better. Often this leads to their making fewer agreements, and to making much better agreements because they intend to keep the agreements they make.

When coaching executives, we regularly ask them to rate their energy in the present moment on a scale from 1 to 10 (1 being low energy and 10 being high energy). Often these executives give a score of 6 or 7. The question we follow up with is this: "Would you be willing to have your energy move up several points?"

If the answer is yes, we ask them a few short, direct questions, one of which is, "Do you have any broken or unkept agreements?" If the answer is yes, we know for certain that this is an energy drain in their lives.

"Are you willing," we ask, "to keep the agreement or clean up the broken agreement?" If the answer is yes, our next question is, "By when?"

At this point, people often think that what we are advocating sounds good, but is unrealistic. "Do you mean I'm supposed to keep every agreement I make? What if things change or things happen?" This question is both realistic and good. That's when we introduce people to the concept of renegotiating agreements.

RENEGOTIATING AGREEMENTS

A simple and unarguable fact of life is that things happen that are out of our control. Despite our leaving on time, an unexpected traffic jam occurs and we end up knowing we won't be able to keep our agreement to be at the meeting at 3:00. It is also true that we change our minds. What seemed like a good agreement when we made it now no longer seems like a good agreement. For these reasons and others, Focus Consulting teaches clients the skill of renegotiating agreements.

The fact is that *broken agreements damage trust.* When we evaluate teams, one of the sure signs of dysfunction is lots of broken agreements. People stop trusting each other to deliver. In our work with high-performing teams, we've seen that trust is a critical component to effective teaming.

Ways to avoid trust breakdowns include:

- Make good agreements.
- Distinguish between agreements and edicts.
- Keep the agreements you make.

Another key to building rather than breaking down trust is to renegotiate agreements as soon as you see that your ability or willingness to keep the agreement is in jeopardy. One of the things that breaks down trust is being surprised or blindsided by a teammate's failure to deliver. Renegotiating keeps people from ever being surprised.

Renegotiating looks like the following examples.

"Bill, I said I would call Johnson at the SEC by 5:00 this afternoon. Dave [the CEO] has asked me to do a project for him this afternoon that I think is a higher priority than the call, so I would like to renegotiate my agreement with you and make the call to Johnson by 10:00 tomorrow morning. Is that OK with you?"

"Kathy, I said I would make 10 sales calls this month to launch our new mid-cap product, but it looks like I will only make 8. I wanted to let you know this in advance so that you wouldn't be surprised at month-end, and to ask if it would be all right if I made 12 calls next month?"

"I made an agreement with the advisory board to produce the new marketing material by quarter end. As I've thought about it more, I think the existing marketing material is good enough given our soft margins and efforts at expense control. I would like to renegotiate the agreement and not do this at all. What do you think?"

This is renegotiating. Notice several things:

- Renegotiating occurs *before* the agreed-upon deadline, not after. The idea is never to surprise your agreement partner by missing a deadline.
- Renegotiating is not about making excuses or explaining. It is simply about stating the facts.
- Renegotiating is a request to change a prior agreement. It is a dialogue, not a monologue.
- Here another pertinent question often surfaces: "What if the other person (especially my boss) won't accept the renegotiation?"

Often this becomes a case of prioritization. We suggest having a discussion with your boss about your current priorities and activities. In the real world, priorities are not static and frozen; rather, they are dynamic. Try saying to your boss, "I can keep that agreement, but I can't keep these other agreements. How would you like me to reprioritize?"

Again, the key from our perspective is *no surprises*. Keeping your teammates informed and in the loop is crucial to effective teamwork.

At Focus Consulting, we take this trust issue very seriously. If we make an agreement to have a meeting at 9:00 AM, and one of us can tell that he or she is going to be 10 minutes late, we call another team member to let him or her know. Quite frankly, this rarely happens anymore, because we have become skillful at making agreements we want to keep and creating enough space in our lives to allow us to keep our agreements easefully. When it does happen, though, we don't want anyone to be surprised by the fact that we didn't show up on time.

Note that we aren't saying it is okay to consistently be late for the weekly staff meeting as long as you call ahead. Repeatedly making agreements that you have to renegotiate will eventually wear down the trust of your teammates. Renegotiation should be the exception on teams that have made a commitment to keeping agreements. In our experience, people who are skilled at impeccable agreements renegotiate less than 10 percent of their agreements.

CLEANING UP BROKEN AGREEMENTS

On your road to becoming impeccable concerning agreements, there will be bumps in the form of broken agreements. You simply didn't do what you said you were going to do, or you did something you said wouldn't do. What do you do then?

On less functional teams, people do the following:

- Act as though nothing happened and hope that no one remembers or brings it up.
- Lie.
- Make all kinds of excuses and blame others. ("The mailroom sat on the document.")

In contrast, high-performance teams handle broken agreements directly and without a lot of drama. They follow these steps.

Face the Fact That the Agreement Was Broken and Acknowledge It to All Concerned

One of the common problems with people we coach is that they simply don't face reality. Instead, they turn away, trying to avoid what is so. Turning away, whether conscious or unconscious, always causes problems. It's like not facing your high cholesterol or your unpaid credit card bill. Unacknowledged issues never just go away; instead, they fester and grow. So too with broken agreements. The first step is to face the fact of the breach and take responsibility. Such a move might sound like this:

- "I agreed that I would hit a sales target of $3 million. I didn't do it. I take full responsibility and want to acknowledge to you and everyone else that I didn't keep my agreement."
- "I said I wouldn't talk to Joan about what you told me. Last night Joan and I had drinks together and I told her what you said."

Usually, facing the agreement lapse takes no more than a sentence or two. The more directly and crisply it is said, the better.

Take Responsibility for the Broken Agreements without Excuses, Justifications, or Explanations

If you haven't read Chapter 3 on taking responsibility, go back and do so now. If you have, you'll understand the concept of taking responsibility for not keeping an agreement. We suggest that you eliminate excuses, justifications, and explanations. By and large, they are a waste of time. Most people are not really interested in our excuses and explanations, and if they are they can ask. If someone asks you for an explanation, you can always give it then.

If you're a parent, think about this. Imagine that your child comes to you and says, "Mom, I didn't clean my room like I said I would. I know we had an agreement and I didn't keep it. I take responsibility for not organizing my time to get it done."

Of course, most of us would pass out from shock if our kid said something like this. Imagine, though, how different such a statement is from, "Mom, I tried to clean my room but Joey had a big problem with Michelle and I stayed up until midnight talking to him online. My alarm clock didn't go off so I was late for practice and today I have to study for a biology test."

If you're like most parents, you have grown tired of excuses. They don't do much but create drama in your relationships. The same is true in the investment world. High-performing teams stop justifying, excusing, and explaining.

Listen to the Responses of Others (Hear Them Out)

Often when we break agreements, people get upset. Of course they do. One of the keys to cleaning up broken agreements is to stay with someone through the upset. This takes the form of consciously listening and validating someone's story and emotions. With your emotional intelligence tuned in to the other person, you should genuinely listen to him and then say something like, "I know you're disappointed and angry. That makes sense." After giving sufficient time to validating his story and emotions, move on to the next step, in which you ask him if and how you can clean up the broken agreement.

Inquire into What You Can Do to Address the Consequences; Then Do It

When agreements are broken, there are almost always consequences. Cleaning up broken agreements means addressing those consequences and doing what you can to correct the situation. For example, one common consequence of breaking agreements is that we damage trust with our teammates. We suggest saying something like this if you have broken an agreement: "I'm wondering if my not keeping my agreement with you about confidentiality has damaged your trust in me and if there is anything I can do to rebuild that trust?" Such a question is an invitation for your teammates to check in with themselves and see if trust has been damaged and then, if it has, to think about what you need to do to rebuild trust.

Sometimes the consequence is that the person who was counting on you to keep your agreement is not able to keep an agreement she made with someone else. Cleaning up the consequences might mean that you take 100 percent responsibility and contact the third parties and let them know that your failure to keep your agreement has made it difficult for other agreements to be kept.

Often just taking responsibility for the broken agreement, without excusing and defending, combined with listening to the other person, is enough to clean up any consequences of the broken agreement.

Handle the Source of the Broken Agreement to Avoid Repetition

Whenever an agreement is broken, we encourage you to get curious about the breach and derive all the learning you can from the situation. Often people spend unnecessary time in guilt, remorse, shame, and self-deprecation. In highly effective teams, we see these as unnecessary and a waste of time. Team members are far better off to get curious and continue learning. A great way to discover the source of an agreement breach and to get all that you can from the situation is to revisit the Clarity Worksheet and answer all the questions on it.

CLARITY WORKSHEET

Our associates Gay Hendricks and Kate Ludeman created an effective tool for developing impeccability about agreements. Over the years, we have seen it produce great results on investment teams that commit to accountability.

> *Exercise*: For one month, use the Clarity Worksheet when making any agreements. At the end of just that one month's practice, our experience is that you will be skillful at making, keeping, renegotiating, cleaning up, and learning from agreements and broken agreements. We often teach teams to "go slow in order to go fast." The idea is that if you go slow for a month and really master the skill of impeccable agreements, it will allow you to go fast in the future because you won't waste time with sloppy agreements and the drama associated with broken agreements (see Table 4.2).

COMMITTING TO IMPECCABLE AGREEMENTS

After reading this chapter, if you are convinced that living impeccably concerning agreements is something that would benefit you and your team, we'd ask you to consider making a commitment, saying it out loud several times and seeing if you encounter any "yes, buts." The commitment we suggest goes something like this:

> "I commit to being impeccable around my agreements, including making good agreements, keeping agreements I make, changing agreements that I want to change, and cleaning up broken agreements."

"I commit to being impeccable about all my agreements."

Remember to honor your "yes, buts" by noticing how you resist making the commitment. What comes up as you think about and voice your commitment? What bodily sensations do you have? Honoring your resistance could simply mean noticing it, breathing with it, and releasing it. We like to ask three questions when someone considers making a commitment:

1. Could I make this commitment?
2. Would I make this commitment?
3. When?

These questions will help you to get clear and to own your commitment one way or the other.

CONCLUSION

How would the meeting of the investment committee that started this chapter have gone if the team had been committed to impeccable agreements? Here are some of the differences:

- If they had had an agreement to start and stop the meeting at certain times, these times would have been honored; people would have been on time, and the meeting would have ended on time.
- If a member wasn't going to be on time, that member would have notified someone.
- If a member had arrived late, he or she would have taken responsibility, taken a few moments to clean up the broken agreement, and gotten the learnings about how he or she was living life around a schedule.
- The analyst covering the service sector and the CIO would have had a clear and concise discussion about the issues related to ServiceMaster, because they would have had a clear agreement from the previous meeting that had been written down.

TABLE 4.2   The Clarity Worksheet

1. We agree that _____ [action agreement] will happen by/at _____ [time agreement].
2. _____ takes responsibility for certifying completion.
3. We agree to make any change in the agreement by direct communication, mutually agreed upon.
4. Initialed and agreed to by _____.

Fact/Feeling Check

I make it safe for myself and others to speak freely about any feelings and facts. As I make this agreement, I'm aware of:

☐ Anxiety, fear, nervousness

☐ Irritation, anger, aggravation, resentment

☐ Discouragement, sadness, resignation

☐ Excitement, happiness, exhilaration

☐ Other feelings

☐ Significant facts:

_____

_____

_____

If failure occurs, we agree to review the reasons and identify our learning edge, doing our best to take 100 percent responsibility and avoid blame.

Reason Check

☐ I failed to estimate accurately the time/resources necessary to complete.

☐ I failed to communicate relevant facts and/or feelings.

☐ I made the agreement with no intention of keeping it.

☐ I made the agreement to please _____.

☐ I made the agreement to get _____ off my back.

☐ I forgot we had an agreement.

☐ I "couldn't" do it because _____.

☐ I was afraid to say at the time because _____.

☐ I changed my mind and failed to tell you.

☐ I didn't realize you were serious.

☐ You "made" me agree to it and I hid my feelings about that.

☐ Not keeping agreements is one of my patterns of self-sabotage.

☐ Not speaking relevant facts and feelings is one of my patterns of self-sabotage.

☐ Other [list]

_____

_____

_____

- The team would have confirmed the time and place, as well as roles and responsibilities, for the upcoming meeting with the client; there would have been no confusion or drama about the situation.
- The CIO would have made a clear request to the entire team about watching CNBC. The team could either have entered into a conscious agreement using the Clarity Worksheet, or the CIO could have been clear that he was issuing an edict. Either way, there would have been a lively discussion, because the team would have practiced the behaviors of candor and conscious listening.
- Finally, no one would have talked about anyone else behind their backs. *No gossip.* Issues would have been dealt with clearly and directly.

We know this replay of the original meeting is a much more effective way to live and run an investment firm because we have seen it happen with our clients time and time again. Weekly two-hour meetings are now accomplished in only one hour, because everyone honors their agreements and time is not wasted on the drama of "he said/she said." Trust levels among the team members are maximized and agreements are rarely renegotiated because everyone is following the steps to making and keeping good agreements.When you compare this real-life scenario with your own meetings, ask yourself which one you want to attend next week!

SUMMARY

- Reminder: Accountability = 100% responsibility + clear agreements.
- There is a clear distinction between an agreement and an edict:
  - *Agreement*—anything I have said I will do or anything I have said I won't do; bilateral.
  - *Edict*—unilateral dictate or instruction.
- The three steps to making good agreements are:
  - Only make agreements you really want to make and that you feel fully aligned with when you make them.
  - Only make agreements about things you have control over.
  - Record your agreements.
- Renegotiate agreements that are in jeopardy; do so before the due date, and without explaining or blaming, in a two-way conversation.
- Clean up broken agreements immediately using the five-step process.

NEXT STEPS

- Review the Impeccable Agreements Self-Assessment Quiz you took near the beginning of this chapter. Are your answers still the same?
- Decide if you are personally ready to commit to being impeccable about your agreements. If so, make your commitment.
- Make copies of the Clarity Worksheet and put them in various places for quick reference:
  - Your portfolio flap—to follow the questions when making agreements in meetings.
  - Next to your phone—when making agreements over the telephone.
  - Next to your keyboard—when making agreements via e-mail.
  - At home—when making agreements in your personal life.
- Review your current outstanding commitments and determine if they are all under your control. If there are some that are not under

your control, renegotiate the agreement to include only those factors under your control.

- If you made the commitment to be impeccable about your agreements, in 30 days retake the Impeccable Agreements Self-Assessment Quiz. Are any of the answers different?
- Make it standard practice for the last agenda item of every meeting to be an explicit review of all agreements made during the meeting: Who will do what by when.
- Introduce the members of your team to impeccable agreements, including the Self-Assessment Quiz and Clarity Worksheet. Ask them if they want to commit to being impeccable about their agreements.

CHAPTER 5

Candor
Revealing, Not Concealing

Jim Ware

If you think it, say it.
—Ray Dalio, President, Bridgewater Associates

Were sitting in the "Long Horn" conference room in a resort with a group of senior executives from a southern money management firm. The group had recently been recognized by *Institutional Investor* for its outstanding record. The Focus Consulting Group was called in by the CEO because, despite his firm's obvious success, he was concerned about the "soft" side of the business. Its human resources department had conducted rigorous focus groups on the subject of trust and found that the junior staff had some concerns. As we interviewed the senior staff, we found that trust issues had surfaced within their leadership team.

At this offsite, we began with our usual process of creating a safe and highly constructive environment in which to have discussions on sensitive issues. We explained the concept of learning agility and "playing above the line" and got agreement from the participants that they would commit to this behavior during the two-day offsite. We then explained our view of accountability, including taking 100 percent responsibility for results. Participants pushed back with some good analytical questions about this behavior, which we addressed, and eventually they bought into the usefulness of this concept as well.

We presented the third leg of the "safe and constructive environment" stool: candor. This is where we hit major resistance. In fact, one of the participants said, "No, I will not agree to be candid." When asked why not, he said, "I don't believe other people will be candid, so I'm not willing to commit to that." During a break, he said, "I believe that I'm the only one who has really been candid so far at this offsite, because I spoke honestly and openly about my unwillingness to be candid." I had to stop and admire the wonderful paradox in that statement.

In our experience, candor depends on trust. If trust is weak within a team, candor will be also. Hence, it was really no surprise that the group in our example was reluctant to be fully candid, as they had already confessed to trust issues. Top-performing teams experience high levels of both trust and candor.

Candor is defined as "openness, frankness, straightness."[1] It is one of the top-ranked values to which investment firms aspire. This should come as no surprise, as most investment professionals—experts in the knowledge business—understand the value of getting all the relevant information on the table and into the discussion. In our daily experience with investment professionals, candor does not involve problems of dealing with bold-faced whoppers (for example, outright lying), but rather dealing with much subtler nuances and degrees of dishonesty, such as withholding information and substituting or mistaking opinion for fact. The very best teams have learned the following four skills and use them to their advantage:

1. Separating fact from opinion.
2. Revealing, rather than concealing, opinions.
3. Holding opinions lightly.
4. Using language that supports candor.

SEPARATING FACT FROM OPINION

One key skill in practicing candor is learning to separate fact from opinion. Facts are unarguable truths: "A minute contains 60 seconds"; "The ticker symbol for Southwest Airlines stock is LUV"; "There are 50 states in the United States." One way to think of facts is that you could say them to the Supreme Court Justices and receive no resistance: all of them would agree. As lawyers say, they would stipulate to the facts.

Opinions, in sharp contrast, are arguable. Statements such as "Joe is a poor team player" (one can just imagine Joe arguing his side of this one!) or "Microsoft stock is undervalued right now" are clearly debatable. The human mind is constantly forming opinions, judgments, interpretations, and evaluations, often based on insufficient evidence—that's just the way the human mind works. (We like the term *story* to capture all of these concepts, as in "My story is . . . .") Behavioral finance has clearly documented this phenomenon of the creative mind. A person watching a coin being flipped sees four heads in a row and immediately forms an opinion that the next flip will be tails. Eyewitnesses to a car accident will give completely different accounts of what happened and swear that they are providing the facts. When I was a mediator in the court systems, I used to hear statements like the following all the time:

Landlord: "It's a fact that the tenant never informed me of his intention to vacate the apartment during our conversation on August 12."

Tenant: "The truth is that I did tell the landlord on August 12 that I would move out on September 30."

As directly conflicting as these statements sound, I am convinced that if you hooked up both parties to lie detectors, you would see that both believe they are telling the truth. In other words, neither party is intentionally lying; each is holding fast to his *interpretation* of the truth.

Here's the important point for high-performing teams: Top teams learn to differentiate fact from story and then to hold their stories lightly. In other words, learn to acknowledge that your story is just that: a story. You don't know if it's true. The problem is that many investment professionals have learned that success depends on their showing a high level of confidence to clients and consultants. Therefore, we instinctively flex our mental muscles and endeavor to make our story sound true to all listeners.

This is a genuine dilemma, and we've been asked about it more than once. "You mean I'm supposed to say to clients, 'It's just my story that Microsoft will be a good investment, I don't really know for sure.'?" Our response is that these teaming skills are designed for internal use with your immediate team. You use them with teammates who understand them and commit to them. You may or may not find complete candor appropriate for use in the world outside your firm.

REDUCING DRAMA IN THE WORKPLACE

The biggest benefit of learning to distinguish fact from story, and then holding your story lightly, is that it reduces drama in the workplace. Most *drama*—defined as going "below the line," resulting in conflict, shouting, arguments, and emotionalism—occurs because two people are battling over whose story is right. Much corporate drama would evaporate if team members could learn to use language such as, "Here's my story about what happened . . . ." Merely using this kind of language helps people to remember that it's just their opinion, not the Truth with a capital T.

Another benefit of the fact/story distinction is superior analysis. Teams that get good at identifying facts and then getting all their stories on the table create better reality maps. As Jack Welch said, "The team that sees reality the clearest wins." Because no one person sees reality completely clearly, but rather through the lens of his or her own biases, it is a tremendous advantage to collect everyone's partial view of reality and then fashion from the fragments a more complete view. This skill requires clarity and courage: clarity, in that people must understand and be able to articulate their view of reality; courage, because often the breakthrough ideas are the least popular and subject to the most skepticism.

A fascinating research study done by Asch on group behavior highlights the natural human tendency to follow the crowd, even when the facts clearly indicate otherwise.[2] In this study, participants were asked to identify which of three lines of significantly varying length—a, b, or c—most clearly matched the length of a fourth line, x. For several rounds, all participants around a table correctly identified the matching line. Then Asch started the experiment in earnest by coaching all participants except one to identify the wrong line of the three candidates. The study was intended to see what the lone, uncoached person's reaction would be. Would he or she go along with the wrong answers to avoid embarrassment? Or would that person speak up against the crowd? In 33 percent of the trials, the lone persons went along with the wrong answers, despite what their own eyes were clearly telling them. Never underestimate the power of the herd instinct!

Most team members, consciously or unconsciously, will sabotage their own efforts to participate candidly if they suspect that their contribution is out of favor with the group or the leader. Therefore, leaders must continually show appreciation of and reward members who display true candor. Some of the best leaders we work with use methods such as always speaking last, so as to combat this strong tendency not to go against the grain.

EXPOSING THE ELEPHANTS IN THE ROOM

We worked with a fixed-income leader who had instituted an attribution system for his analysts so that each analyst's contribution to the portfolio could be measured. This leader's intentions were clearly noble: he wanted to have accountability on his team and he wanted year-end bonuses to accurately reflect each member's contribution. The problem, in the eyes of the analysts, was that this system tended to pit them against one another. In confidential interviews, we learned that several analysts had withheld vital information from colleagues because it would have improved the colleagues' performance at the information provider's expense. Although we don't have a dollar amount, the analysts' description indicated that serious money was lost because of the attribution system.

The point of the story, as it relates to candor, is this: The leader was completely unaware of the problem because none of the troubled analysts had told him, "I'm concerned about the attribution system. It seems to be creating a conflict of interest between personal rewards and firm success." In fact, when we told the leader what we had learned in these interviews, he was shocked. He had had no idea that the attribution system was anything but positive. In a high-performing team that practices candor, one or more of the analysts would have shared their concerns with the boss, who would then have had a more complete picture of reality on which to base his decisions. (He might still have instituted an attribution system, but at least he would have done it from an informed and conscious position.)

The attribution system in this example was what we call "an elephant in the room." Elephants are big problems, typically stinky ones, that are simply ignored. Chris Argyris, mentioned earlier in this book, calls these problems "undiscussables": They should be addressed and resolved, but they aren't. In the very best firms that we work with, the leaders have created sufficient trust and candor levels such that during our confidential interviews we don't discover any elephants in the room. We do discover unresolved issues, but they are not hidden. Senior and junior staff members are aware of them and are working toward solutions. Leaders such as Larry Gibson at Thompson, Siegel & Walmsley, Harin da Silva at Analytic Investors, and Kim Redding at K.G. Redding & Associates come to mind as examples of executives in firms where no elephants were mentioned during Focus Consulting interviews with the staff.

A COMMON LANGUAGE ENCOURAGES CANDOR

To review, high-performing teams separate fact from story; hold the latter lightly; and have the courage to reveal, rather than conceal, their stories. In all of this, language is important. We encourage team members to say, "My story is . . . ." Simply using this language reminds the speaker and others that what is being related is a story, not the capital-T Truth. If someone seems to be pounding a story over his or her teammates' heads, it's useful for someone to ask, "Are you holding this story lightly?" Usually this question alone will spark laughter from the group, especially if the pounder clearly has had a death grip on the story. Again, a common language is key to successful application of the skill.

Another phrase we find useful is, "I'm having the thought that . . . ." We believe that many ideas occur spontaneously, without our trying to make them happen. For example, while listening to a CFO describe an earnings scenario for a company, you might think, "No way, they'll never earn that." This thought isn't a carefully reasoned response, but more of what we call a *blurt*. Your mind just reacted and blurted up a thought.

During meetings with teams, we often encourage them to just blurt out their reactions to a topic or statement. We think blurts are wonderful examples of candor—as long as they are held lightly. For this reason, we use the language suggested above, "I'm having the thought [for example, a blurt] that . . . ." The implication of this language is that the thinker isn't necessarily committed to what she's thinking, but that it flashed across her radar screen.

One of the more entertaining blurts that I recall from our experience with clients occurred during a telephone call with the CEO of a rapidly growing investment firm. This firm had grown from a handful of employees and a few hundred million dollars under management to nearly 100 employees and several billion under management. The CEO had called us because he was aware that the firm's culture was breaking down under the stress of growth. They had rapidly hired skilled people to fill roles without careful thought as to the appropriate fit with the firm's culture. To his credit, this CEO knew that culture had become a serious issue and was addressing it. Our role was to help define the culture and build a high-performing team. In this regard, the CEO used one of the funnier analogies we've ever heard concerning our consulting business: "We'll take everything you've got . . . just back your truck up to our offices and dump it all in." We still chuckle at that image.

During our interviews with this firm's employees, we found more than a few elephants in the room—in fact, we found various life forms strewn all over the environs. Trust and candor had suffered greatly during the high-growth period. Morale was low. Again, to his credit, the CEO was genuinely committed to building a strong culture and to remaining open and curious rather than defensive and closed.

The amusing candor story occurred early in our relationship with this firm, before we really got to know, appreciate, and like the CEO. During our initial interviews with the senior staff, we heard from three different staff members that we should get our consulting fee up front because the CEO might not pay us. Of course, this triggered our use of the Rule of Three, explained earlier in this book: If you hear something only once or twice, you can probably safely ignore it, but if you hear it three times, you'd better pay attention. In this case, three people mentioned payment of our fee as a concern.

One of the things I like most about working with Jim Dethmer is that he truly walks the talk. More than anyone else I know, he lives according to the behaviors described in this book. Thus, it shouldn't have surprised me when he said to the CEO, "I'm having the thought that we may not get paid for this engagement." (At this point my mind silently blurted, "Oh great, we can kiss this engagement goodbye!") The CEO was understandably taken aback and asked Jim to explain, which he did, saying that this concern had come up several times during our interviews. After the initial awkwardness and Jim's explanation, the CEO asked what kind of a response he could give to Jim's blurt. Jim responded, "I have a request that we get paid for our work." Another powerful and simple tool is turning concerns and complaints into requests. The CEO found that request eminently reasonable and agreed.

We have, ever since, had a very good relationship with this firm, and have developed great admiration for its CEO, who continues to learn, grow, and develop his leadership skills as he builds a strong culture. Together, we laugh about the early bit of candor just described, but candor has improved significantly among the senior team and is rewarded and appreciated in this firm.

Firms that practice candor tend to experience few surprises. A simple metric for measuring the excellence of a leadership team is the number of surprises that arise. In the same sense that Wall Street does not like earnings surprises (unless of course they are positive!), employees do not like surprises in their performance reviews. It should never happen that an employee is shocked by feedback about bad performance. Good managers are "current" in providing feedback; that is, they deliver the news in a timely and direct fashion. Just as I was reviewing the material for this chapter, I dealt with two phone calls from leaders who had surprised portfolio managers with bad news. In one case, the CEO had sugar-coated performance reviews so that the person in question was completely surprised by the final decision to fire her. The CEO's lack of candor caused a major surprise. A second phone call was from a portfolio manager in the Midwest who was shocked that she had not received the nod for the top job in the firm's succession plan. Again, in firms that practice excellent candor, these surprises are eliminated or held to an absolute minimum. Instead, what we see in many firms is reflected in the University of Oklahoma study, cited earlier in this book, that one in three business interactions involves a lie. Not a bold-faced whopper, but a misdirection, as seen in these two cases.

CANDOR IN THE INVESTMENT PROCESS

Seated next to Ted Truscott, CIO of Ameriprise Financial (formerly American Express Financial Services), I was listening to a team of analysts and portfolio managers present and debate the merits of investment scenarios. This was a drill that Gordon Fines of New Dimensions Advisors had devised. Analysts would present a buy idea and a sell idea. Portfolio managers then would ask questions and critique the presentations. At the end of the day, awards would be given to the analysts with the best presentations. All of this took place during an offsite (held in May 2005) designed to sharpen the skills of the team; no money was actually being invested.

Ted is familiar with the behaviors that we teach—above and below the line, accountability, and candor—and said to the team at the end of the day: "I want to appreciate you all for the hard work that you put into preparing these presentations. And for the good debate that you engaged in." Then he paused and specifically referred to the behavior we've been discussing: candor. "However, I think you could have pushed each other more. I think you avoided the really tough questions. We need to continually improve on staying above the line but also being absolutely candid in our discussion of investment ideas."

Our way of thinking about top-notch communication is captured in the curiosity skills (above and below the line) and the candor skills. The latter includes the skill of delivering the truth in a tactful way so as not to provoke defensiveness. (For example, if you want to clear the air with a colleague, you can preface the conversation with, "I'd like to discuss something with you with the intention of improving our business relationship . . . ") On the other side of this message, the receiving side, the person can practice curiosity and openness in the face of feedback. Teams that work both sides of this exchange get very good at quick and effective decision making.

As a way to practice candor, Chris Argyris has designed a simple but powerful exercise. While sitting in an investment meeting, take a sheet of paper and draw a line down the middle. On the left-hand side, note what comments came to your mind that you did say out loud. On the right-hand side, note the thoughts that you withheld; that is, they occurred to you, but you chose not to voice them. You will be surprised at how many thoughts you censor. The Rule of Three applies to candor as well. If you censor a thought three times, assume that it's important enough to say out loud. Trust that there is a reason why your mind keeps bringing this thought back to your awareness.

Candor requires courage. It helps to use the language that we've suggested ("I keep having the thought that . . . "). Again, you may not know why a particular thought recurs. In our experience, though, both internally and with clients, it's best to trust that there is a reason and have the courage to reveal rather than conceal.

SUMMARY

- Candor is one of the top-ranked values to which investment firms aspire.
- Candor is closely linked to trust. If trust levels are low, candor will suffer as well.
- The best teams have learned to:
  - Separate fact from opinion.
  - Reveal, rather than conceal, opinions.
  - Hold opinions lightly.
  - Use language that supports candor.
- The top investment teams will embrace the challenge of practicing candor and raise the level of their game accordingly.
- Candor helps eliminate surprises.

NEXT STEPS

- Practice using the language of "facts" versus "stories." Agree with teammates that you will distinguish these during meetings. For example, if a team member says, "It's a fact that all of us are hard workers," agree that someone will jump in and say, "Excuse me, but that's your *story*."

- How do you and your teammates mislead each other?
- How do you and your teammates withhold from each other? For a month, try the exercise of drawing a line down the center of your notes page. Then record what you actually said on the left and what you thought of but didn't say on the right. See if any of the "withholds" occurs three times or more. If so, ask yourself why you are unwilling to share this thought with the team.
- Does your firm's culture emphasize being nice over being direct? Do you deliver the hard information accurately, in a timely fashion?
- Do you collude with team members who deceive themselves about performance or agreements or deadlines?
- With whom do you most need to clear the air? Will you? When?

◆

CHAPTER 6

Authenticity
Eliminating Drama

Jim Ware

The most respected and trusted leaders are basically the same whether they are in the middle of a strategy meeting or hanging out in their pajamas.
—David Tittsworth, Executive Director,
Investment Adviser Association

D rama occurs at all levels of most corporations. Investment professionals who work in an office with more than two people don't have to flip on the afternoon soap operas to get their daily fill of drama. We consider living and working authentically to be the antidote to corporate drama. Therefore, this chapter is really about eliminating drama from the workplace.

One way to define *drama* is simply to say that it is what occurs when team members or entire teams go below the line. (Remember the discussion in Chapter 2 about curiosity versus defensiveness? Defensiveness is "going below the line.") In every case, when someone gets defensive and goes below the line, that person has taken on a *persona* (the term is from the Greek word for "mask"). In other words, the person has, usually without knowing it, put on a mask and begun playing a role defined by "predictable patterns of mostly unconscious behaviors triggered by a few basic instincts common to all of us."[1] For example, while doing 360-degree interviews for a portfolio manager, we found that several of his direct-reporting staff used the same words to describe his defensive behavior:

"He becomes Mr. Know-It-All." We call that a persona: It's a predictable role that he assumes under pressure.

All of us develop personas during childhood. We discover that we'll get attention and praise from our parents if we are smart or funny or well-behaved or helpful, so we become the know-it-all or class clown or goody two-shoes or helper. Personas that are largely positive are labeled Level One personas. If Level One personas don't completely work—for instance, our parents don't fully give us the attention or praise we seek—we often develop Level Two personas. These are also life strategies for getting what we want, but they have a more negative quality; for example, the rebel or the bully or the smart-ass.

The impact of personas can range from mildly annoying (say, that of the smart-ass) to seriously destructive (e.g., the bulldozer). One of the most destructive cases of persona warfare I've seen occurred at the ownership level of an otherwise successful money management firm in the Midwest. The two owners had been working together for 17 years. One was the president responsible for day-to-day operations at the firm; the other was the CIO who designed the investment process and chaired the stock selection committee. The issues between them had come to a head after 14 years of working together. Because of their differences, the relationship had become so dysfunctional that the two of them rarely spoke during their time in the office. One of the leaders knew of our work with investment firms and asked us to help. We interviewed both the leaders and their senior team of analysts and portfolio managers. We found a common theme running through all the interviews: The president of the firm had taken on the persona of the critical parent, while the CIO had become the rebellious teenager. When we explained the notion of personas and suggested to the leaders that they were acting out the roles of critical parent and rebellious teenager, neither took exception. In fact, they agreed that the description we offered accurately summed up their relationship for the last three years.

The resolution to their conflict depended on each of them taking 100 percent responsibility for their parts in creating the drama at the firm. They had both been playing below the line for nearly three years. Unfortunately for the two owners, their employees, their clients, and probably their families as well, the owners were unwilling to take full responsibility, shift back above the line, and resolve their differences. They each maintained that the problems were largely the other person's fault. As a result, the lawyers are now determining how to divide a multi-billion-dollar investment firm. Personas can be powerfully destructive if unrecognized and unresolved. Consider the list of common personas in Table 6.1 and find the ones that are familiar to you.

When working with a team of investment leaders, we sometimes ask them to identify themselves and then ask the rest of the team to pick a

TABLE 6.1 Common Personas

Accommodator	Harried Harry/Harriet	Pollyanna Good News
Action Jackson	Have No Opinion	Poor Me
Adventurer	Head Honcho	Procrastinator
Armed and Dangerous	Hermit	Prophet of Doom
Blamer	Hip Shooter	Quiet One
Boss	Hunker Down	Rant and Rave
Bulldog	I'll Do It My Way	Rebel
Bulldozer	I'm Outta Here	Resister
Bully	Jack Hammer	Rescuer
Chameleon	Joker	Resigned to Whatever
Chess Master	Juggler	Responsibility Avoider
Complainer	Just Do It	Savior
Conflict Avoider	Know-It-All	Scorekeeper
Contrarian	Little Red Hen	Screamer
Control Freak	Land Mine	Shredder
Cowboy	Last Minute	Sly Cat
Crab	Lone Ranger	Smart-Ass
Credit Seeker	Loose Cannon	Space Case
Critic	Martyr	Stressed Out
Cynic	Me Too	Stealth Bomber
Do-It-All	Micromanager	Suicide Bomber
Drama Queen/King	Milquetoast	Trickster
Dr. Efficiency	Misunderstood Genius	Tyrant
Dreamer	Mole	Uninvited Fixer
Drill-Down	Name Dropper	Wait and Pounce
Eager Beaver	Observer	Warrior
Energizer Bunny	Overwhelmed	Watchdog
Glory Seeker	Peacemaker	Wire Brush
Goody Two-Shoes	People Pleaser	Wheeler-Dealer
Grudge Holder	Perfectionist	Worrier
Hammer	Politician	

persona for each of the other team members. More often than not, the personas selected by an individual and the ones selected for him by the group are similar. This group exercise of increasing the team's awareness around personas is useful because it is precisely the tool of awareness that is most helpful in defusing the power of personas.

For example, we work with one CIO who has a dominating personality. After doing this exercise and getting labeled "Steamroller" by a number of analysts, the CIO began jokingly to refer to himself in the same language. Once, during a heated debate, he started laughing and said, "Here comes the steamroller and I'm afraid I can't stop it!" The room erupted in laughter and the mood lightened considerably. In the absence of this kind of insight, the debate would have devolved into the old battles, which left a toxic residue for days afterward.

An important aspect of each persona is the underlying noble intention. As we write this book, we're working with two fixed-income directors for two separate firms, who have been accused by their teams of being control freaks. In one case, the portfolio involved is a short-term cash management vehicle that, if mismanaged, could literally bankrupt the entire firm. Therefore, the fixed-income director keeps daily tabs on it, for obvious reasons. What we find common to both control-freak managers is a sincere desire to get it right and make sure all the details are carefully considered.

In this sense, personas are a bit like old software programs in need of upgrades. At one point in life, the persona was the most effective way to get what the mask-wearer wanted. Now, a new software program may be available that greatly enhances efficiency and is free of the negative, toxic effects of the old persona. For example, we've seen control freaks become accountability coaches who excel at inspiring commitment and ownership in projects. They learn how to teach accountability to their direct-reporting staff in a valuable way rather than simply terrorizing them, at worst, or annoying them, at best.

PERSONAS: A PERSONAL EXAMPLE

The concept of personas was extremely helpful in my early days as a research analyst. Working for Gary Brinson and following the financial industry, I was responsible for understanding and modeling the earnings streams of companies run by the likes of Hank Greenberg, Sandy Weill, and Phil Purcell. Pushovers, right? As part of my research, I met and interviewed these leaders. Here's where I learned a valuable lesson about personas, although it would be years before I learned the term *persona* or studied the works of experts such as Hal Stone or Gay Hendricks.

Because I was a young analyst, the interviews with these lofty leaders of the financial world created a predictable level of anxiety in me—and any time anxiety is present, the odds are good that a persona will pop up. Remember, they are the old software we developed to cope with anxious moments. My predominant old software was the "Friend of Mankind" program. In my family of origin, being nice usually served to keep me out of harm's way. So, predictably, when I went into these interviews with tough, intimidating CEOs, I would ramp up my Friend-of-Mankind persona to about level 10. I was the friendliest SOB on the planet!

The problem with this tactic was that this old persona was both inappropriate and counterproductive. These CEOs were running a very different program, called Punch-Counter-Punch. They had risen to their success levels by being tough negotiators and smart strategists. In their minds, when an analyst entered their office for an interview, an intellectual boxing bout started; the gloves went on and the bell sounded. The way to earn their respect was to spar with them for as many rounds as you could before they inevitably knocked you senseless. This is all very clear to me now, with 25 years of hindsight. I have to chuckle at the images I retain of my first interviews: I must have looked to them like a mixture of Mr. Rogers and Will Rogers, flashing a warm, toothy smile and waving a little sign that said, "I never met a man I didn't like."

One big trouble with personas is that they're not very creative. This is a major reason why we encourage teams to become conscious of their personas and shift out of them, for increased creativity. When I was in my Friend-of-Mankind persona, and it wasn't working (which, believe me, it didn't with the likes of Hank Greenberg!), all I knew as a backup strategy was to do more of it. This behavior—more smiling and friendliness—further puzzled and frustrated the interviewee CEO, who was looking for a good intellectual sparring partner, not a friendly dog on its back exposing its belly for vigorous rubbing. Their response usually was to ramp up the bulldozer persona. Round and round we went: me getting friendlier by the minute and the CEO getting fiercer by the minute, friendlier, fiercer, friendlier still, fiercer still. Very quickly, I created a victim-and-villain scenario, which is the topic of the next section.

Before turning to the topic of the Conflict Triangle, though, I will note that eventually I understood the dynamic just described. I wish I had known about personas earlier, because it would have saved me a lot of embarrassment and grief. However, I did figure out that the Friend-of-Mankind persona did not serve me at all well in CEO interviews. I eventually learned to keep that old software on the shelf and to bring out the appropriate character, whom I named "Sherlock" after the famous detective. Sherlock was a worthy adversary for the CEOs and wasn't at all interested in befriending them. Sherlock continues to be useful to this day, as we work with and advise the same kind of CEOs who used to terrify Mr. Friend of Mankind.

THE CONFLICT TRIANGLE: VILLAIN, VICTIM, HERO

As people become familiar with personas and accept the concept as useful, we at Focus Consulting Group introduce a central tool for resolving conflict in the workplace: the Conflict Triangle. In Chapter 2, on curiosity, we described the concept of going below the line, and here we can provide more detail. *Going below the line* means entering into drama and conflict. Whenever we hear during interviews that the organization is experiencing lots of drama and conflict, we can bet that the employees involved are showing up in personas that fit into one of three meta-persona categories. In other words, all of the personas listed in Table 6.1 can be categorized in one of these buckets:

1. **The Villain**. Personas that fit here are typically Critic, Bulldog, Bulldozer, and Control Freak. The Villain points a finger and asks, "Who's to blame for all this?" Blaming can escalate into attacks and result in people diving for cover when the Villain appears. The noble intention of Villains is usually to excel and get the work done efficiently and thoroughly. The big fear of villains is loss of control.
2. **The Victim**. Common personas here include Poor Me, Overwhelmed, and Worrier. Victims are at the mercy of someone or something; life

just happens to them. Common statements from a Victim are, "It's no use, the system will never change" and "I can't say that to the boss!" Victims see themselves as powerless. They often talk about how horribly and unfairly they've been treated. They need someone to be the bad guy so that they can be righteously indignant. They usually don't look for their own contribution to the problems at hand. They also have the noble intention of getting the job done, but sabotage it with the assumption that doing so is not within their power. The big fear of victims is loss of safety or security.

3. **The Hero**. Hero personas include Helpers, Peacemakers, and Fixers. At first glance, you might say, "Those are good things, right?" Not necessarily. Heroes are overfunctional. To use our language from Chapter 3, on taking responsibility, Heroes are taking more than 100 percent responsibility. They often step in, uninvited, to solve another person's problem. Like the co-dependent spouse who allows his or her partner to continue drinking, gambling, or overspending, Heroes protect people from facing and fixing their own problems. Their noble intention is to protect and take care of people who are in trouble. The big fear of heroes is loss of approval.

One pension plan that we worked with did a feedback exercise in which they identified the personas, triangle position, and noble causes for each member of the senior team. The overwhelming triangle position for all team members was Hero. This exercise provided clear evidence that everyone was being a little too nice, avoiding conflict, and smoothing over all disputes.

Figure 6.1 shows the meta-personas—Villain, Victim, and Hero—with characteristics of each.

Once you are aware of the Conflict Triangle and start to look for it, you'll find it frequently. While meeting with the CEO and CFO of a successful asset management firm in Sydney, I asked if they had the "right people on the bus." (This is one of our favorite—and critical—first questions for any leader.) The two of them thought for a minute and agreed that they did, with the possible exception of one person. He was a highly talented portfolio manager whom they labeled "difficult." When I drilled down into the meaning of *difficult*, they said he often got defensive when challenged and usually responded by going on the offensive. In

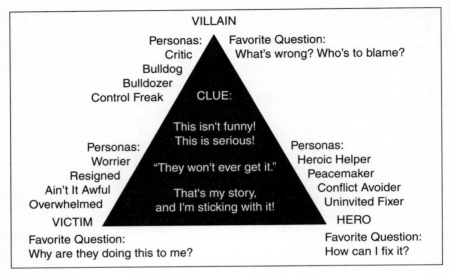

FIGURE 6.1   Conflict triangle.

short, he shouted and bullied people. The CFO, a woman, said that she felt threatened by him and would often freeze up when he went into his bully routine. Within the first five minutes of talking to these leaders, whom I'd only met via one telephone conversation, I realized that they were describing two personas of a classic Conflict Triangle: the Villainous bully portfolio manager and the Victim CFO. No sooner had this thought occurred to me than the CEO, in classic Triangle fashion, jumped in and said, "I've had to intervene several times when this portfolio manager has become too belligerent." Enter the third persona: the Hero.

I remember chuckling and saying to these two bright and successful leaders, "You're stuck in the classic Conflict Triangle." I then explained the Triangle and the role that each of them was playing. They nodded in agreement and asked the logical question: "How do we get out of the triangle?"

GETTING OUT OF THE TRIANGLE

The best way to stay out of the Conflict Triangle is not to get into it in the first place. This can be done by paying attention to when you go below the line; that is, get defensive. (Remember the defensiveness scale introduced in Chapter 2?) When you can catch yourself early in the game of getting defensive, you have the opportunity to shift back to a state of openness and curiosity, using a reliable shift-move as discussed in the chapter on curiosity. We get into the Triangle when we miss that opportunity and go further into defensiveness.

Getting out of the Triangle requires an understanding of the model—the roles of Victim, Villain, and Hero—and the ability to notice when you have taken on one of these roles. In this sense, moving out of the Triangle means that you pay attention instead of operating on automatic pilot. It means that your emotional intelligence must be adequate to notice when you have become angry, fearful, or sad; also, your body awareness must be sufficient to tell you that some part of your body has become tense. Thus, the first step out of the Triangle is awareness: being able to say clearly, "I am *in* the Triangle."

As with all our processes, the next step is a choice to shift out of the Triangle or to remain in it. This may sound like an odd step: wouldn't we always want to shift out of the Triangle? One hopes that for you, the answer is usually yes. There are times, however, when a person is so strongly in the grip of a persona—so stuck in the Triangle—that the honest answer (we're big on honesty) is, "No, I don't want to shift." They want to bitch, moan, complain, shout, whine, whatever.

In this case, the persona user may need to use the strategy of playing it up big. To loosen the grip of a persona, an effective strategy is to exaggerate the role, ham it up, and play it out to the max. (I do this with my "misunderstood genius" persona. I'll march around the house, complaining and shouting, sometimes followed by my wife and our dog. We invariably end up laughing so hard we hold our sides . . . well, not the dog.) If the feeling underlying the persona is big—big anger or sadness or fear—try playing it out. When you feel and express it, the energy in the persona will be released. (The classic release move is beating on pillows to release anger—it works!)

If, in contrast, you are in the Triangle but your feelings are moderate, you may choose just to shift, to simply step out of the Triangle. In most situations, especially at work, this will likely be the case (unless you and your work colleagues have created a really high-drama situation). If so, you can catch yourself operating in the Triangle and simply choose to shift. Here are the steps for shifting out:

1. Take full responsibility for whatever is upsetting or bothering you.
2. Wonder about how you created or fueled the situation.
3. Explore the underlying familiar pattern in whatever is occurring.
4. Express your feelings without blaming anyone or anything.
5. Shift above the line—into curiosity—about what you need to do to create more ease and effectiveness.
6. Brainstorm solutions.
7. Take action and keep your commitments to the solutions.[2]

Another strategy that we've employed concerning the Triangle and resolution of corporate drama is called the *persona interview*. The idea behind this tactic is to learn more about the persona. In other words, the interview is intended to find out more about why someone developed this particular strategy for getting things done or getting what he wants. As we become more familiar with these parts of the psyche, they lose their grip. The script and instructions in Table 6.2 can be used by someone conducting a persona interview.

One of my mentors, John Lee, has written 11 books on the subject of

TABLE 6.2   How to Conduct a Persona Interview

Person A interviews Person B; then they can reverse roles.

Step 1: Person A: What is the name of this persona?

Step 2: Person B shifts into character and responds with a name that fits (for example, "The Driver" or "Poor Me").

Person B steps fully into this persona as if he or she were putting on a suit of clothes. Act it out. Ham it up. Assume all the body postures and mannerisms this persona takes on. Use props if you wish.

Step 3: Interview this persona. Person A asks these questions and Person B responds.

1. [*Name of Person B's persona*], what's the most important thing to you?
2. _____, what are you most proud of?
3. _____, when did you make your first appearance?
4. _____, who did you learn your style from (parent, sibling, grandparent, teacher, coach)?
5. _____, what are you most afraid of?
6. _____, what do you most want?

personas and shifting from below the line to above the line. He is an expert on the topic of emotional intelligence and skills such as expressing anger safely and appropriately. He has developed a related, skillful process for shifting, and has taught it to thousands of people with great success.

The following is his description of how to shift from being in the Triangle (below the line) back to your authentic (for example, grown-up) self:

> You ask the person what they are feeling or thinking as they begin the process.
>
> Ask them what this experience; circumstance, person, or place is reminding them of from their recent or distant past.
> Ask them what they would have liked to have said or done back then and then encourage them to express this verbally (and if trained to do so, express it physically).
> You ask them what they would have liked to have said or done to them in the past.
> You ask them how they are feeling now.
> You ask them what they need to say or do in the present.
> It is important to note that all of these are questions. Adults tend to ask other adults. Regressed men and women [for example, below the line], who are drowning in their histories, their fears and anxieties, tend to make statements full of assumptions and advice.
> After doing the process the person usually takes a deep breath and sighs which is a physical cue that says, "I'm back to my adult state."
> The person usually feels and expresses gratitude to you for being safe enough to do the process with them and for you seeing their feelings and not judging them.
> While there have been no "scientific" studies done, I have asked hundreds of people how they feel after using this process. Ninety-nine percent say better, great and thank you for seeing me and hearing me.[3]

We use a similar process with our investment clients, and I'm pleased to report that they have had similar results.

BENEFITS OF ELIMINATING CORPORATE DRAMA

Most of our work boils down to energy. As Einstein showed us, everything is energy. Teams locked in drama and conflict exhibit low energy. In fact, these people are often exhausted at the end of a work day. At one firm, which is in the running for "most dramatic workplace in the investment industry," a portfolio manager told me over coffee that the stress level had become so high that people were manifesting physical symptoms. She said, "I've started losing my hair, another colleague has colitis, another one was diagnosed with an ulcer, and the list goes on." You can't imagine a whole lot of creativity occurring in a setting like that. In fact, since we had that conversation, the confidante manager has quit the firm without another job offer. She just chose mental and physical health over that toxic work environment. Table 6.3, created by my colleague Jack Skeen, is a good way for individuals and teams to measure their energy levels.

The top firms that we work with have managed the drama and conflict to create truly creative and productive teams. At Ariel Capital, for example, John Rogers and Mellody Hobson have committed to eliminating the drama and conflict in their organization. They've examined themselves, asking the question, "How do I help create drama or conflict in this organization?," and they've taken this work to the senior team and the junior staff as well. They have devoted entire offsites to the topic, believing that a high-energy workplace will give them a competitive advantage for years to come. Mellody Hobson, Ariel's president, stated that "with the help of Focus Consulting Group, we have learned how

TABLE 6.3 Energy Level Measurement

	1	2	3	4	5
Personal	Hanging on by my fingernails	Sliding slowly	Holding my own	Learning and growing	Excited, energized, creatively engaged
Team	At each other's throats	Tolerate each other	Silos but productive	Cooperate reasonably	Seamless cooperation, fun, high productivity

drama creates negative energy that is divisive and stifles creativity and success. We are committed to eliminating it from our environment so that a spirit of teamwork and collaboration can enable us to maximize our results as well as our relationships."[4] For readers who don't believe that the "soft stuff" (for example, leadership and culture) affects the "hard stuff" (for example, bottom-line results), here is a list of recent accomplishments for Ariel:

- Ariel Fund tops the list of the USA Today All-Star Mutual Fund Team.
- Ariel Appreciation Fund was named to Morningstar Fund Investor's Focused Ten.
- Ariel Fund and Ariel Appreciation Fund received 4-Star Overall Morningstar Ratings and earned "A" Morningstar Stewardship Grades as of June 30, 2005.
- Ariel Capital Management was recognized as the largest minority-owned asset management firm in the country. The firm has received this recognition annually since 2002.[5]
- Ariel Capital Management ranked 13th among money managers for new business won.[6]

SUMMARY

- Authenticity (getting real) is the antidote to corporate drama.
- Drama is created when we become defensive, go below the line, and adopt personas to deal with the pressure.
- Three common personas and behaviors—Villain (blaming), Victim (complaining), and Hero (rescuing)—are often found together in corporate drama, and together create the Conflict Triangle, which can be difficult to break.
- Getting out of the Triangle requires emotional intelligence and the willingness to shift out of a persona into a more effective approach.
- Teams that have effectively and consciously managed drama and conflict can create truly creative and productive teams that enjoy higher energy levels and greater success.

NEXT STEPS

- Which personas live in your firm? Pusher, Critic, Know-It-All, Accommodator, Micromanager, Overworker?
- Which personas create problems in your work culture? How can these personas change so as to contribute to performance? That is, what is the underlying noble intention for each?
- Which personas in your firm do you really dislike? Examining this is very useful. Almost always, the personas that we really dislike are actually parts of ourselves. Hence the saying, "If you spot it, you got it!"

  Example: An Accommodator may really dislike a Bulldozer because the Accommodator has "disowned" the assertive part of his own personality.

- Make an active intention to discover your three most-used personas over the next month. Keep a record and at month end be able to say, "Most often I become (1) ____, (2) ____, and (3) ___."

CHAPTER 7

Awareness
Using Emotional and Intuitional Intelligence

Jim Ware

If you don't know who you are, the market is an expensive place to find out.
—Adam Smith

Awareness means learning to use your whole self—not just your logical mind—to absorb and process information, and make decisions. Tuning into your body, emotions, and intuition can provide valuable input that the logical part of your mind cannot give and does not even recognize. Like each of the behaviors described in this book, awareness challenges the conventional thinking in the investment world, though this chapter may be more radical than any of the others. Conventional thinking of investment professionals asserts: "Emotions hinder performance. If we could only get rid of these pesky emotions, our investment performance would improve." The idea is that emotions cloud our thinking and spoil objectivity.

Behavioral finance reinforces this notion with countless studies of our predictable, irrational behavior, mostly based on fear. These days, neuroeconomists—researchers who combine cognitive neuroscience, psychology, and economics—have taken the argument a step farther with statements like the following:

> A new study shows people with brain damage that impaired their ability to experience emotions such as fear outperformed other people in an investment game.

- The brain-damaged participants were more willing to take risks that yielded high payoffs
- They were less likely to react emotionally to losses
- They finished the game with 13 percent more money than other players.

We beg to differ. Though we find the studies from behavioral finance and neuroeconomics fascinating and useful, we stand firmly in the camp that says emotions and intuition are resources that will greatly improve decision making and teamwork in an investment firm. We would not recommend lobotomies for investment staffs. In fact, neither would neuroeconomists:

> Yet emotions may play a useful role in financial decision making. While the brain-damaged players did well in the specific game in the study, they didn't generally perform well when it came to making financial decisions in the real world. Three of four of the brain-damaged players had experienced personal bankruptcy.[1]

This chapter explores why it is important for world-class investors and their teams to think with their whole bodies; that is, relying on both emotions and intuition. We use the word *awareness* to capture the general idea behind whole-body thinking.

If we could use the latest medical equipment to study analysts and portfolio managers, I'm sure we'd find that the most active parts of their brains (the parts that were being used most heavily) were the left hemispheres. Most investment professionals still rely heavily on the analytical resources of the mind. They read, think, design spreadsheets, apply mathematics, talk to experts, and then do it all again. The still-prevailing wisdom in the industry is that (1) emotions hurt decision making and (2) logic and facts trump instinct and hunches any day of the week.

Research on thinking and decision making has become increasingly sophisticated. Although most investment professionals rely primarily on the analytic skills of the left brain, evidence now shows that there are other important resources for decision making: the right brain (big-picture, creative thinking and pattern recognition); the limbic brain (the emotional and oldest part of the brain, which scans the environment for threats and sounds alarm signals); the body itself (which can express itself through tight chest, back pain, increased heart rate,[2] lump in the throat, etc.); and, of course, intuition.

Though they would never do so in earshot of a client, investors acknowledge that intuition accounts for much of their success. I've stopped counting the number of analysts and portfolio managers who confess to me that their research reports are nothing more than a formal justification for what they "know" is the right investment decision. In other words, they did what Malcolm Gladwell calls "thinslicing."[3] They took a quick look at a situation and got an intuitive hit that it was attractive, then they put together a case supporting that recommendation.

Increasingly, all these bodily and nonrational sources of information are being recognized as potent allies in the game of investments. After all, we need every advantage we can get in making world-class decisions!

The stakes become even higher, though, when we move from investment decision making to building high-performing teams. Many individuals in the investment world are shocked when they move from the role of individual contributor (say, an analyst for a fixed-income or equity fund) to the role of team leader or team member who is expected to interact skillfully with other members of a team. Once the game changes from intellectual analysis to team dynamics, emotional intelligence far outweighs the effect or utility of intellectual intelligence. In fact, research by the Center for Creative Leadership suggests that emotional intelligence is more important than IQ or experience at the job by a factor of three to one.[4]

So what exactly is emotional intelligence? The leading name associated with this term is that of Dan Goleman, author of *Emotional*

Intelligence and its sequel, *Primal Leadership*.[5] Consider this research from Goleman, who analyzed nearly 500 competence models of leadership from top companies:

> The higher the rank of those considered star performers, the more emotional intelligence competencies emerged as the reason for their effectiveness. When the comparison matched star performers against the average ones in senior leadership positions, about 85 percent of the difference in their profiles was attributable to emotional intelligence factors rather than to purely cognitive abilities like technical expertise.[6]

Compare that statement with the assertion by a CIO of a major insurance firm: "If given two candidates for investment leadership positions, one with investment knowledge and the other with general leadership abilities, I'd pick the investment expert every time." This position is common in the industry; essentially, it states, "We need to be led by one of our own."

Though we don't completely disagree with the idea that investment knowledge is crucial to a leader's success, we believe that the top firms recognize and act on the idea that their leaders need to have both technical and leadership expertise. A key attribute of successful leaders in the asset management world is their desire to lead. Jane Marcus and Terry Bacon made this point in a paper entitled "Developing Better Asset Management Leadership":

> This is an industry where, historically, no one wanted to be the leader. Leadership hasn't been rewarded or valued. The best people were often more motivated to be a salesperson or a portfolio manager, where the rewards were greater and more predictable and where, frankly, there was more energy and psychic satisfaction. To many talented people, shaping a business has been far less interesting and rewarding than shaping a portfolio. Furthermore, many people are attracted to asset management because it is analytical and rational, rather than interpersonal and emotional. Some people who might otherwise make good leaders simply don't like the messy challenges of dealing with people issues and problems.[7]

This last point reminds me of a comment from a portfolio manager who was participating in Focus Consulting Group leadership training. When we made a similar point about messy people issues, he responded with refreshing candor: "That's why I chose investments—I don't like dealing with people!" Many investment professionals agree; they don't like dealing with people issues. Nevertheless, great danger for leaders and top-performing teams lies in ignoring precisely those issues. As the saying goes, "Denial is not just a river in Africa."

There are investment leaders who get genuinely excited about the challenges of leadership and building a winning culture. One such leader is Michael Sapir, CEO of ProFunds in Bethesda, Maryland. Sapir founded the company in 1997 with a handful of employees and a vision to democratize investment opportunity through developing and offering custom index funds. By 2005, the firm had grown to more than $6 billion in assets and nearly 80 employees. Sapir has turned his attention to building a first-class culture that attracts and retains top people and allows them to develop and use their individual gifts. He has a genuine interest in leadership and a humility that allows him to remain open to improvement and coaching. A lawyer by training, he is a very skilled debater, but has also learned the skills discussed in Chapter 2 on curiosity: the ability to remain open and curious.

Another such leader is Kim Redding at K.G. Redding & Associates in Chicago. A leader in the real estate investment trust (REIT) business, Redding is committed to both first-rate performance and building a first-rate culture. Like Sapir, Redding manages his ego so that he remains curious and open to learning. Both men have considerably enhanced their native emotional intelligence skills.

But again, what is emotional intelligence? Emotional intelligence has four basic components, which can be divided into two major areas:

Personal Awareness

1. Self-awareness—being able to identify one's emotions and recognizing their effect on others.
2. Self-management—being able to manage one's emotions so as to reduce defensive and unproductive behaviors.

Social Awareness

1. Social awareness—sensing other people's emotions; reading people.
2. Relationship (social) management—skillfully combining the three preceding components to build trust in relationships, resolve disputes, and inspire cooperation and teamwork.

SELF-AWARENESS

Don is a highly skilled and successful research director in the fixed-income field. His team has established an excellent performance record, outperforming its benchmarks by significant amounts and ranking in the top decile of managers. Despite this successful record, the team's future is threatened by the departures of three key players, all of whom attributed their departures to Don's leadership style. Specifically, one of the departed analysts said, "He micromanages and intimidates. I don't deny that he is smart and knows the industry but he's arrogant. And it's all about him. When the numbers are good, he wants much of the credit. When they're bad, he points fingers."

We were brought in to give Don 360-degree feedback from his peers, create a development plan for him, and coach him. In usual investment fashion, the leaders wanted this done by lunchtime. The feedback and development plan can be done in short order, but successful coaching requires a commitment from the individual and several months for the changes to stick. Goleman elaborates on this in his work on emotional intelligence:

> The limbic brain (for example, the emotional brain) is a much slower learner—particularly when the challenge is to relearn deeply ingrained habits. This difference matters immensely when trying to improve leadership skills: At their most basic level, those skills come down to habits learned early in life. If those habits are no longer sufficient, or hold a person back, learning takes longer. Reeducating the emotional brain for leadership learning, therefore, requires a different model from what works for the thinking brain: It needs lots of practice and repetition.[8]

Most investment professionals make the mistake of thinking that when they understand the concept behind, say, choosing curiosity over defensiveness, the game is over. They've got it. They understand it . . . but doing it is far more difficult. (Imagine someone listening to a lecture about weight loss and saying afterward, "That makes perfect sense; okay, I'll drop 50 pounds over the next few weeks.")

The feedback for Don revealed that his emotional intelligence was low. He had survived and thrived using his left-brain, analytical skills. When it came to awareness of his behavior and its effect on team members, though, almost every co-worker and direct-reporting staffer answered, "He's not aware of his own weaknesses or how they impact others." In the debriefing session with Don, after we had collected data from 10 co-workers, we explained the principle of choosing curiosity over defensiveness. We also told him that we would check in periodically and ask, "Are you feeling open or defensive as you hear this feedback?" As we stated earlier in this book, this skill of noticing when one is defensive is hugely important to management success.

Before we started the actual debriefing, we asked how Don was feeling in general. His answer was, "Good." This response is characteristic of many investment professionals. They respond to this question with "good," or "fine," or "okay," or "peachy," or similar words. What we point out is that none of these responses describes a feeling. Rather, they are judgments. (In the show, *Defending the Caveman*, the author plays on this pervasively accepted stereotype that men have low emotional intelligence. The protagonist's wife claims that he doesn't know what he's feeling. He considers this for a moment and then, with conviction and pride, says, "I know what I feel: I feel like watching TV!") Words like "good" or "fine" or "watching TV" don't describe feelings. Terms for feelings are different; they describe an emotional state.

There are four basic feeling categories: anger, sadness, fear, and happiness. Feelings reside in the body. People with high emotional intelligence can tune in to their bodies and tell you, at any given moment, what they are feeling. The answer doesn't reside in the brain; feelings are not concepts. We pointed all this out to Don and asked him to pick one of the four. This time he said, "Fear." This made perfect sense. After all, he was about to get a bucket of feedback poured over him, much of it negative. How could he *not* feel some fear?

As we progressed through the session with Don, we continued to check in with the question, "Are you feeling open or defensive?" Each time I asked the question, Don responded before the sentence was fully out of my mouth: "Fine, I'm open." We typically find that the faster someone responds that he is fine, the more defensive he actually is. In contrast, people who are truly open usually pause, take a breath, scan internally for a second, then respond with a thoughtful, "I seem to be open." One investment leader who modeled true humility and candor in this regard was John Rogers at Ariel. While doing a feedback exercise with his team, in which his assignment was to identify whether he was open or defensive in response to feedback, he answered in a thoughtful way nearly every time, "I'm defensive." This allowed the rest of the team to feel comfortable admitting their own defensiveness when their turns came around.

It's important to understand that Don was not trying to be deceptive in any way about his feelings or his defensiveness. In other words, he wasn't trying to purposely mislead us about how he was feeling. Rather, he was largely illiterate in the language of feelings, and not particularly internally sensitive. Most men, and many women, too, are in the same boat. With the exception of emotional extremes (for example, "Did you see what that driver did?! I'm so pissed off, I could scream!"), most people are largely unaware of how they feel.

In Don's case, his low emotional-intelligence quotient (EQ) had seriously affected the success of his team. Though they readily acknowledge his expertise and industry knowledge, every one of them said that he was largely unaware that they were all afraid of him. He used his knowledge to bully them. Many team members said that they felt diminished in his presence. When we presented this feedback to Don, he was shocked; he had been completely unaware that his team felt this way.

To give another practical example of why it's important to have emotional intelligent or "literacy," let's switch to the investment committee of a large equity mutual fund. The portfolio manager is listening to input on a position from the analysts seated around the table. After a few minutes of listening to one analyst, the portfolio manager begins drumming his fingers. After a few more minutes, he interrupts loudly and angrily, "Enough already, we already had this debate about pricing in the industry and I don't agree. I think pricing is going up." The result of this eruption is that the analyst in question and all the others around the table slide down a few inches in their seats, pulling their heads into their shells.

While facilitating this meeting, we noticed a pattern: The portfolio manager in question usually started drumming his fingers long before he finally let the analyst know that he'd heard enough. It became evident that he would let the analysts speak long after he'd made up his mind. Then he would erupt, setting a defensive tone for the remainder of the meeting. Therefore, we coached him on being more attentive to his internal barometer of when he had heard enough. By tuning in to himself, he could cut a conversation off earlier, when he was still calm, without biting someone's head off.

Before moving on to the second skill or component of emotional intelligence, self-management, here is a continuum for each of the four major feelings. It's useful to be able to identify where you are at any given time on these scales (see Table 7.1). Importantly, at any given moment, we are always feeling *something*, however slight. High emotional intelligence means that we can recognize and identify the feeling.

SELF-MANAGEMENT

Self-management depends on self-awareness. If we don't know what we're feeling, we can't manage those feelings effectively. Sometimes we do know what we're feeling, but we manage them poorly anyway. For example, one portfolio manager with whom we work tells the story of losing his cool and costing his firm a significant amount of money. He had just found out that one of his largest equity holdings was in the news for cooking the books. He had worked closely with the firm's CFO in the last few months to learn about this company's business, accounting, and prospects. When he learned of the fraud, this portfolio manager went bal-

TABLE 7.1 Continuum of Emotional States

Frustrated	Angry	Enraged
Worried	Scared	Terrified
Mopey	Sad	Grieving
Content	Happy	Ecstatic

listic. He felt personally insulted, even violated. He stormed into the trading room and told the traders to sell every share he owned, driving the price even lower than the 20-percent decline of the day. The following day, the stock did the proverbial dead-cat bounce and regained 10 percent. A rough calculation shows that waiting even one day would have saved the firm several hundred thousand dollars. That's the cost of poor self-management in actual dollars.

Of course, there are other costs as well. Angry leaders who don't know how to cool themselves down can create a toxic environment that drives out top talent. In one case we know of, a derivatives trader was so fed up with the boss's rantings that he quit in the first week of December. Colleagues reminded him that if he stuck it out until year-end, he'd qualify for a sizable bonus. His response? "It's not worth it"—and he left the same day. Many of our coaching assignments involve talented portfolio managers whose behavior drives analysts out of the firm. It's good to remember: People join firms but they leave managers.

SOCIAL AWARENESS

This skill involves the ability to read people. One of Don's weaknesses, as described in the initial example, was his almost complete inability to empathize with other employees. He had very little idea of how they were feeling, especially in relation to his actions and decisions. For example, Don was the leader who instituted an attribution system for measuring individual performance by analyst. Don's intentions were good: he wanted to create better accountability within the team and to reward analysts who made good selections.

The problem with this type of attribution strategy, which we described in Chapter 5 on candor, was that it created a conflict of interest, because it pitted the analysts against one another. However, none of the analysts gave Don this feedback, because they feared him. When we told Don, it turned out that he was completely unaware (1) that the analysts feared him, and (2) that they disliked the attribution system in its present form.

People with high emotional intelligence can read the body language and facial expressions of others and can usually tell if something is amiss. When leaders ignore this ability or let it atrophy, they endanger their effectiveness. Much like a ship that has lost its radar, they are vulnerable to sneak attacks. (My colleagues Jack Skeen and Jim Dethmer have unusually well-honed gifts for reading people. Recently, Jack and I were sitting across from a CIO who was struggling to give a clear "yes" to our question, "Do you want to be coached?" After a pause, Jack said, "You want the CEO to be coached as well, don't you?" The CIO leaned forward and nodded. Jack's intuition was spot-on.)

RELATIONSHIP (SOCIAL) MANAGEMENT

The final skill of emotional intelligence puts all the pieces together. The ability to identify and manage one's own feelings and to read and empathize with others allows a leader to manage and motivate the team. Social management allows investment leaders to skillfully manage smart people who basically don't want to be managed in the first place. As Marcus and Bacon stated, "Asset management leaders must be able to work with strong egos and independent personalities."[9] One of the most useful skills that an investment leader can master is simply the ability to *listen well* to the differing points of view on her team. Human beings have a deep need to be heard and understood. Even hard-driving, independent, brilliant investment pros still need this from their bosses. Whenever the Focus Consulting Group works with a team in conflict, we first create a "reality map" on the wall of a conference room, to list all the differing viewpoints on an issue. Leaders who take the time to carefully listen and record all the views will be rewarded with an immediate lessening of the tensions. Why? Because the real need, for most people, is simply to be heard and understood, not necessarily to get their way. Hence, a powerful step in calming people down is to create a reality map.

A second instance in which social awareness is critical is the vision process. Leaders are responsible for creating compelling visions. We've witnessed leaders at both ends of this spectrum, from truly inspirational to starkly demotivational. The simple fact is that most investment firms exist to provide superior investment performance. Therefore, results are often the core of an investment firm's mission statement. Good leaders go beyond that, reaching for a vision that will motivate and inspire their teams.

In the summer of 2005, we had the pleasure of listening to Marc Mayer, chairman of Alliance Bernstein's research efforts, deliver a presentation to the team. It was one of the best motivational speeches I've ever heard. He knew his audience—logical, analytical, introverted, brilliant researchers—and he knew how to appeal to their sense of excellence and pride. He began by removing his 90-year-old wristwatch and describing its amazing precision and timelessness. "This watch," he said, "will still be working, with proper care, 100 years into the future." His point was that Bernstein's research has set the standard for precision and excellence in the industry research. He showed audience members a model of causation, starting with global, innovative research and ending with the client's peace of mind. By taking this line of causation all the way to "peace of mind," he successfully completed what we call the Four Whys exercise. In other words, he kept answering, for each piece in the model below, the question "Why is that important?"

Global Innovative Research >
  Knowing More >
    Using Knowledge Better >
      Achieving Long-Term Results >
        Peace of Mind

He did not end the chain with long-term results (for example, alpha, Sharpe ratios, information ratios, or excess returns). He did what good leaders do and went for what underlies it all: *the client's peace of mind.* He addressed the ultimate "why," the "so what" question.

Mayer then told stories about the research culture at Bernstein. These included stories about CEO Lew Sanders, who holds legendary status as one of the world's greatest researchers, and media analyst Tom Wolzien, who discovered broadband technology as an investment vehicle before the term *broadband* was even coined. Mayer was clearly proud of Bernstein's heritage and was telling wonderful stories to help the junior analysts understand the culture of the firm. Thorough knowledge of his audience allowed Mayer to highlight the aspect of Bernstein that would most motivate the up-and-coming analysts: namely, Bernstein's clear reputation for outstanding research. He showed them the data from industry surveys, which rank Bernstein number one in all of the following categories of research:

- Quality
- Industry knowledge
- Detail
- Trust
- Originality
- Challenging management
- Best company studies
- Useful valuation framework

If Mayer had stopped there, he still would have had the minds and hearts of those in the room. But he knew how to deliver the complete package, so he moved next to Bernstein's 30-year record for alpha contribution. The firm has delivered, on average, hundreds of basis points per year in outperformance in its flagship services. This sort of excellence has won Bernstein, and its parent, Alliance Capital, over two-thirds of the top 50 pension plans as clients.

Combine the material that Mayer presented with his clear emotional involvement—he was obviously very proud of Bernstein—and his sense of humor, and the result was an outstanding pep talk for savvy professionals. The point is that Mayer had to be able to access his own feelings of excitement and pride, or he couldn't have designed and delivered such a wonderful speech. The analysts gave him the highest rating of any speaker that day.

FEELINGS IN THE WORKPLACE

Now that you're aware of feelings—both your own and those of others—what do you do with them in the workplace? The answer is so simple as to be laughable: *Just feel them.* Feelings, if uncensored and unedited, will pass through the ordinary person like wind through the branches of a tree. If you don't believe this, just watch a group of preschoolers playing. They will laugh, cry, get angry, and return to laughing all in the course of five minutes. I know from watching my two- and four-year-olds, especially in their interactions with each other, that feelings just flash through them. Feelings are like energy currents running through the wiring of our bodies. If the channels are unblocked, the emotions just run their natural course. In contrast, blocked energy, like a dammed-up river, can cause powerful and damaging eruptions.

Medical science is beginning to make the link between unfelt and unexpressed feelings and physical illness. In one study, for example, a group of people were instructed to write about an important issue in their lives, while another group copied names from a telephone book. The latter group—the control group—experienced no significant physiological change during the experiment. The former group experienced a decline in blood pressure, an increase in functioning of the immune system, and other physical benefits.[10] Allowing feelings to surface and be felt, as in the writing exercise, is beneficial to clear thinking, good physical health, and high energy levels.

This information is not new. Knowledge of the connection between expression of feelings and health, thinking and energy, goes back centuries. The modern version of these ancient findings has been formalized and taught by people such as Gay Hendricks (*Conscious Living*), Gene Gendlin (*Focusing*), and John Lee (*Regression*). All these approaches advocate acceptance of whatever feelings arise.

Note, importantly, the difference between *feeling* and *accepting* an emotion and *acting* on it. This is the crucial distinction in emotional intelligence between the first step (self-awareness) and the second step (self-management). Many of us have so thoroughly learned to ignore and suppress feelings that when they do surface, they do so with great intensity. For example, when another driver cuts us off, instead of feeling a simple expression of anger ("I'm mad"), we move right into full-blown rage ("I'm gonna pull that %^&* out of his car and beat the %^&* out of him!"). In this instance, a current event has triggered some old, unexpressed anger that has festered and become rage.

People highly skilled in emotional intelligence know when they are dealing with a current situation and the associated feeling (because the charge of the emotion is usually manageable and low-key) and when they are dealing with something from the "way-back machine." One of the most impressive skills a person can master is the ability to say, in mid-conversation, "I'm sorry, but I need to end this conversation now and schedule a time to continue it." (As we pointed out in Chapter 2 on curiosity, we always recommend this course of action when a person has gone below the line.) When this happens during a conversation that I'm having with one of my Focus Consulting colleagues, I am reminded of how lucky I am to be dealing with highly conscious people.

INTUITION: THE EQUAL PARTNER OF LOGIC

Intuition is another powerful ally for both world-class decision making and world-class team performance. In some ways, intuition is even more mysterious than emotion. The latter can be identified in the body: I'm sad, and I have a lump in my throat; I'm mad, and my neck is stiff; I'm scared, and I have goose bumps. Intuition can manifest simply as a thought, or a hunch, or a solution that appears out of thin air. I remember discussing intuition with Richard Rooney, CEO, and Craig Pho, CIO, at Burgundy Asset Management in Toronto. Burgundy had been involved in some dealings with Enron before Enron's collapse. The Enron representatives had offered Enron stock as a form of payment. The Burgundy team had collectively formed a bad feeling about the experience with Enron and, for no other reason than this intuition, turned the stock deal down.

Leaders like Sapir of ProFunds and Redding of K.G. Redding are convinced that their successes are largely due to their intuitive ability to figure out, with the help of facts and data, what the next right move is. Leaders who operate this way are in good company; as Albert Einstein, arguably one of the greatest minds of the twentieth century, remarked, "The intellect has little to do on the road to discovery. There comes a leap in consciousness, call it intuition or what you will, and the solution comes to you and you don't know how or why."[11]

For this reason, people who work with Sapir and Redding have sometimes been frustrated because they cannot follow the logic of some decisions. Often, as Einstein mentioned, these leaders themselves cannot articulate precisely how they arrived at a solution or decision. Fortunately, their teams recognize that these gifts of intuition, though difficult to explain, have led to great success and excellent track records.

For his book, *The Intuitive Trader*,[12] Robert Koppel interviewed many successful traders on the topic of intuition and how it plays into their strategies. Every one of the traders interviewed agreed that the highest degree of expertise occurs when a person's experience and knowledge allows him or her to move beyond intellect into the realm of intuition. In the words of Bill Williams, a trader of 35 years and author of the book *Trading Chaos*: "At the fifth level, which is what I call the expert level, trading is almost all right hemisphere. It's all intuitive . . . . At this level you know what the right trade is without knowing how you know."[13]

When operating at the highest level, investment professionals must integrate both logic and intuition. Dr. Richard McCall wrote, "The more intellectual your approach, the less you are able to be intuitive and responsive in the moment . . . . The fact is indisputable: when you really do trade well, you really cannot call it mechanical. You must be an intuitive trader!"[14]

The paradox is that good intuition relies on lots of left-brained, intellectual experience and hard work. Edward Toppel, long-term member of the Index and Options Market and author of *Zen in the Markets*, wrote, "Intuition allows you to take advantage of all that hard work you've done."[15]

Actually, the so-called paradox is consistent with the message of this book: *balance*. A superior investor will use all the resources available: left brain, right brain, limbic brain, and all the cues from the body. The mistake that many investors still make is to rely solely on their favorite hemisphere, the logical left side. The purpose in citing all these examples of successful intuitive traders is to encourage conventional investors to experiment with using intuition, so that they will be using all the tools and weapons available to them.

"What does intuitive trading actually look like?," a skeptic might ask. Here is a description from Linda Leventhal, long-term independent trader and member of the International Monetary Market division of the Chicago Mercantile Exchange:

> [S]ome days I'll keep trying to buy the market. I'll be trading in and out from the long side. In other words, I keep looking to buy the market on a break or retracement. All of a sudden, I'll get a feeling and I'll say to myself, this market feels heavy. That's exactly

what I'll say, it feels heavy; meaning it doesn't feel right. I think it's going up. But if I rely on my intuition, my intuition tells me it feels heavy . . . it's more than just a feeling, it's vital information. If my head says buy and I keep trying to buy and it isn't working, and all of a sudden my stomach tells me it feels heavy, I will rely on my intuition. I'm going with my stomach! Most times I won't be able to even verbalize it. It just happens automatically. Experience has taught me to trust it.[16]

Some professional investors might react to this line of reasoning with, "Yes, but long-term investing is different from trading; therefore, we shouldn't take our cues from them." Although there are differences between trading and investing, the main difference is the time frame. The key to success is still decision-making ability. The master investors[17] all demonstrate the successful interplay between logic and intuition. Clearly, hedge-fund legend George Soros, with his penchant for reversing huge positions on a moment's notice, relies heavily on his intuition. Even Warren Buffett, the exemplary long-term investor ("My preferred investment horizon is forever"[18])—uses intuition in his investing. He is well known for doing major business transactions only with people whom he trusts. In this sense, Buffett relies heavily on his intuitive ability to size up the character of business partners. The facts and logic—both left-brain matters—could help Buffett eliminate certain potential partners (the ones with shady records), but they could never confirm that someone would be trustworthy in the future. A leap of faith, based on intuition, is required for that.

Intuition also allows today's portfolio managers to operate more quickly, without assembling all the available information. Legendary investor Charles Merrill (of Merrill Lynch fame) commented on this phenomenon. He said that "[i]f he made decisions fast—intuitively?—he was right 60 percent of the time. If he took his time and analyzed a situation carefully before reaching a decision, he would be right 70 percent of the time. However, the extra 10 percent was 'seldom worth the time.'"[19]

The business leaders who run the major companies in which portfolio managers invest are also recognizing the importance of intuition. Bob Galvin at Motorola is a good example: His intuition told him that wireless communication would be a gigantic opportunity for the future, although he had no strong data to support this. After a long battle with a skeptical board, Galvin prevailed. The company redirected its efforts into one of the most profitable industries of the century.

Cutting to the chase, two researchers—John Mihalsky and E. Douglas Dean at the New Jersey Institute of Technology—examined the impact of intuition on the corporate bottom line. (Let's get serious; after all, as investors, isn't that what we *really* care about?) They found that 80 percent of the CEOs whose company profits had doubled over a five-year period were found to have above-average intuitive powers.[20] The explanation for their success? Intuitive people, as Einstein recognized, possess superior insight. They can reach solutions by leaps and bounds rather than waiting for all the data to be analyzed. Given the speed at which business changes these days, this trait ranks as one of the single most important assets. In a contest that's as hard to win as investing, doesn't it seem odd that players would handicap themselves by ignoring this entire resource? Peter Senge at MIT put it this way in his best-seller, *The Fifth Discipline*: "[Leaders] cannot afford to choose between reason and intuition, or head and heart, any more than they would choose to walk on one leg or see with one eye."[21]

As the investing public gets wiser and more money goes into passive funds, the squeeze may be on. Investment firms will have to offer real value. They won't be able to bluff Joan Q. Public. She'll be focusing on results, not complicated theories and brilliant excuses. The intellectual smoke and mirrors, albeit impressive, won't matter. The majority of firms will have to face—and deal with—the fact that they can't consistently outperform the benchmarks. The band will stop playing and Joan will take her punch bowl and go home.

When that happens, maybe, just maybe, we'll see some cracks in the armor of the intellectual fortress. Out of necessity, investors will begin to explore the full range of thinking resources that are at their disposal; not just the analytic left brain, but the right brain, limbic brain, and entire body as well. Sound farfetched? George Soros's son said of his famous dad:

My father will sit down and give you theories to explain why he does this or that but I remember seeing it as a kid thinking, at least half of this is bull. I mean, you know the reason he changes his position on the market or whatever is because his back starts killing him. He literally goes into a spasm, and it's this early warning sign.[22]

SUMMARY

- Awareness means learning to use your whole self, not just the logical part of your mind, to absorb and process information and to make decisions.
- Mind, body, emotions, and intuition all provide valuable input.
- Research shows that in moving from intellectual analysis to team dynamics, emotional intelligence is far more valuable than intellectual intelligence.
- Emotional intelligence, which includes self-awareness, self-management, social awareness, and relationship (social) management, requires an in-depth understanding of one's own feelings and an ability to empathize with others.
- Intuition is another powerful ally for both decision making and team performance.

NEXT STEPS

- Pick a day to try this experiment. Set your watch to beep on the hour, or arrange to have an assistant or colleague call you. Each hour, when you get the reminder, ask yourself, "How am I feeling right now?" See if you can become skilled at naming one of the four basic emotions: anger, sadness, fear, or happiness/excitement.
- Where in your body do you carry tension? Shoulders? Lower back? Head? Neck? Can you use this knowledge to design a more easeful working life?
- How would you rate yourself on the emotional intelligence scale (EQ)? In which of the four components are you strong? Weak? What can you do to improve?

- Recall a time when you used your entire body/mind gestalt to make a decision. What were the circumstances? How did this differ from business as usual?
- How do you experience the inner critic in your professional life? In what situations does it get particularly active (making recommendations, working with clients, new situations, etc.)?
- What do you do to soften the tone of your inner critic?[23]
- Who do you know that models integrated body/mind use well?

CHAPTER 8

Genius
Maximizing Your Contribution

Jack Skeen, PhD

The TAP program at Capital Group helps new hires find their areas of genius.
—David Fisher, Chairman, Capital Group

Certainly, one of the greatest and biggest investments every successful financial firm makes is in its people. Some firms conscientiously recruit the best and the brightest from the finest business schools in the country. Other firms seek out the unknown gems from the smaller and lower-profile schools. From various backgrounds, people come to work in our industry knowing that much will be demanded of them, but that handsome rewards will come to those who excel.

A few professionals rise to the top and become nationally acclaimed portfolio managers, analysts, or strategists, earning their reputations with their consistently keen insights and instincts. Others drop out. They either can't keep up with the lightning-fast pace, don't have the savvy necessary to survive, or choose to apply themselves in a different field, for a variety of reasons.

The majority of professionals in the investment industry, however, live out their careers somewhere on the continuum between the extremes of icon and dropout. What determines where an investment professional will land on that continuum? Our experience in working with thousands of employees in the investment industry indicates that success and satisfaction are highly correlated with how well your job responsibilities and firm's culture fit your natural abilities.

WHY JOB DESCRIPTIONS FAIL

The typical approach to matching people with tasks is the traditional job description. With input from the hiring manager, someone in human resources compiles a list of duties and responsibilities for each position. A candidate is matched with an open position based on education and past experience. A career is born!

The weakness in this model is the lack of precision in degree of fit between a person's natural talent, the job description, and the environment in which he or she will work. Imagine buying a pair of shoes just by size alone. Try it sometime. A size 7 in one style is too big, while the same size in another style is too small, or too narrow, or has too high an arch. The only way to get a comfortable shoe is to try on numerous pairs until you find the one pair that fits. All the others will only create discomfort.

It is easy to see that many people have positions that are too big here or too tight there. They simply aren't a right fit. The symptoms of a poorly fitting job are obvious:

- Procrastination—tasks that you put off, or take much longer to do than is necessary.
- Mediocrity—things you simply don't do very well, yet are part of your job.
- Boredom—temptation to read the newspaper, visit the washroom, surf the Internet, or shoot the breeze with a co-worker.

The degree of fit is predictive not only of degree of success, but of job satisfaction as well. The hallmarks of a fulfilling career are to be so excited, engaged, and challenged by your work that the day flies by, leaving you with more energy than when you started that morning.

GENIUS: YOUR PLACE TO SHINE

The key to finding the perfect job fit is the concept of genius. Your personal genius is your unique collection of natural gifts and talents. By *genius,* we do not mean that you are better or smarter than anyone else. Rather, your genius defines where you are at the top of your game, the best you can be, your place to shine.

Our experience has clearly taught us that genius belongs to everyone. Those who excel in life are those individuals who understand their genius and live and work in that space rather than forcing themselves into roles outside the scope of their natural gifts and talents.

Warren Buffett has genius as a portfolio manager. Is this an accident? Is it luck? Was he simply in the right place at the right time? Or did he find his perfect fit early in life and follow that path faithfully? In fact, Warren Buffett was a paperboy as a child—but not a typical paperboy. He tried to cover more than one route at the same time. He started playing the stock market at age 11. In high school, he started his own business and used his profits to invest in Nebraska farmland. He recognized his genius early. The signs were clear, and following that path led to greater and greater success.

Buffett's story is a great example of recognizing and following your genius. He learned early what he loved to do. He paid attention to where success came easily and abundantly. He refined his understanding of his genius through his experiences until he understood his "sweet spot," that place where his natural talents, temperament, instincts, and creativity all came together. Then he stayed there and worked from that spot, building his life around his genius.

It is important to distinguish genius from success. Although genius usually leads to success, many other roads lead there as well. In addition to success, some of the signs of genius are a deep contentment, an honest modesty, and a lack of restlessness in those who are committed to their genius. We have worked with many industry leaders who have had tremendous personal and professional success, yet lack any sense of peace. Despite their success and financial wherewithal, they experience a persistent anxiety that all they have attained will suddenly disappear. They are obsessed with the outward signs of their success: social status, public and professional recognition, a residence in the "right" neighborhood, and belonging to the right clubs.

Contrast such restlessness with Buffett's attitude. He seems a little awed by his own personal wealth. He lives a modest life, as evidenced by the fact that he still lives in the first house he ever bought. Clearly, his joy is in doing what he loves to do, not in doing it for some other end. (Buffett once commented on his career satisfaction, saying, "I tap dance to work each day!"[1])

Another sign of genius is the desire to do what you're doing forever. Those whose careers are not a great fit long for the day they can do something else. They plan to hit it hard, and to create enough success that they can retire early. Such people live as if they were holding their breaths through some of the most wonderful years of their lives.

People who find their genius rarely want to retire. They love what they do and hope to keep doing it in some form or fashion for the rest of their days. As the years go by, they might adjust their hours to fit declining energy, but they will be in their particular game as long as they have breath. It is simply too much fun to quit!

Buffett is certainly not the only investor to work in his genius. Peter Lynch, Charles Brandes, Bill Miller, Dean LeBaron, Ralph Wanger, and John Rogers, to name just a few, found their perfect fit as well. Nevertheless, many investment professionals we've worked with look enviously on those who have found and work in their genius, because they have very few clues as to how to find their own.

KEYS TO FINDING GENIUS

There are several ways, or *keys*, to identify your genius gifts:

- Success
- Delight
- Creativity
- Ease
- Feedback

THE SUCCESS KEY

Success is a wonderful indicator of genius. Success is the barometer that indicates where your instincts and talents interface with the world in the most productive ways. Think through your history, all the way back to childhood. What have you done that has worked very well?

I have a friend whose financial worth is more than $100 million. He made his money building and running retirement communities. As we looked at his life together, he noticed that he has had the knack of buying low and selling high all his life. He has the nose for the deal—he just does.

Once you know what you do that works, the next step is easy: Do it more, and do other things less. Don't let your time become occupied with bureaucracy, politics, or anything else that distracts you from what you do best. If you are a deal maker, do deals!

When we at the Focus Consulting Group work with clients on succession planning, the most common situation we encounter is that of the investment or technical specialist: someone who has a genius for investment research or portfolio management and has no interest in, talent for, or aspiration to manage people. Many a client has forced such investment professionals to take on people management so they could be promoted, make more money, or be positioned for future leadership. Their companies' succession planning, performance management, and incentive systems did not allow for two separate yet equally valuable career paths: research analyst/portfolio manager *or* team leader. Many of these situations result in terminations (voluntary and involuntary); junior staff who are not being developed by the reluctantly promoted group manager; or demotions, when the group manager begs to be returned to her or his former role as a research analyst or portfolio manager.

In these instances, our first step with the client is to review the concept of genius. Forcing someone to take on responsibilities for which he or she has no natural abilities results in misery, as well as significantly reduced efficiency and success, for everyone.

Take a moment with the following exercise to think it through for yourself and get as clear as you can about precisely what you do that creates the most success.

Exercise:
1. List all your successes in the past.
2. List where or how you experience the most success in your current role.
3. What conclusions can you draw about your genius?
4. What can you do to test your conclusions?

THE DELIGHT KEY

What do you do that puts a smile on your face and a bounce in your step? What a great question! One of the signs of being out of your genius is energy drain. You can't wait for the work day to end. When it is over, you are tired, frustrated, irritated, and grumpy. It is as if the day drained you of vitality and life. If this is your common experience, we can tell you that you have not yet found your genius or that you have not yet committed to living in it.

What are those things in life that delight you, add to your energy, and make it feel as though time is flying by when you are doing them? All of these are indicators of genius. You know you are in your genius when you are so engrossed in what you're doing that you finally notice you're hungry, realize you missed lunch, and know that you don't care. What you are doing simply brings you too much delight to put it down. At the end of the day, you have more energy than at the beginning. You go home smiling, happy, and ready to take on the world.

Exercise:
1. What did you do today that drained you of energy? How can you *not* do that tomorrow?
2. When did you feel delight today? What were you doing?
3. How can you design tomorrow to have delight again?

THE CREATIVITY KEY

Another way to discover your genius is to notice which things engage all of your creativity. You are detached from your genius when you are doing things that you experience as boring, laborious, mundane, and tiresome.

Procrastination is the primary symptom of detachment from creativity. Have you ever found yourself looking at your to-do list and finally starting a task that you have put off over and over? That is a bad first step. At that point, notice how you engage the task.

For example, it should take about an hour to complete this particular chore. As soon as you start, though, you realize that you need to use the restroom. You are back in 15 minutes and reengage the task. A few minutes later, you decide that you're thirsty, so you take a coffee break and end up talking to someone in the hall. You are back in 30 minutes and reengage the task. A few minutes later, it's time for lunch . . . actually, it's a little early, and you really aren't hungry, but you go to lunch anyway. You come back in an hour and again take up the task. Now you have spent two and a half hours and still aren't finished. You put the chore back on your to-do list and push it off to some other day. All these are clear signs of trying to make yourself do what is not in your genius.

In contrast, some tasks are fun to do. You look forward to them. You engage them and drive them to completion. You also just seem to do them better than most other people do. You add your touch, your flare— or, in our language, your creativity.

Creativity is critical to success and satisfaction. It defines what we do differently than others and, hence, where we get the most success and recognition. Also, it is where we engage life most openly and freely, thereby creating for ourselves the most satisfaction and happiness. Working from your genius engages all your cylinders with the opportunities of life. Nothing within you is wasted.

Exercise:
1. List all the things you did today that felt boring or were not satisfying.
2. List all the things you did today that engaged your creativity.
3. Design the perfect job to fit your creativity.

THE EASE KEY

Your genius comes to you easily. It does not take a lot of effort, strain, or drama. I have met many successful people who have just worn themselves out in their efforts to get ahead. They have reached their destination, but at great cost. They have wealth and freedom to do whatever they want, but are unhappy and detached from what they want to do. They are so burned out that they lack the energy or creativity to use the opportunities they fought so hard to secure. It is as if they are hacking their way through a jungle, working hard and covered with sweat, while 30 feet away is a flowing river that winds toward the destination they are working so hard to attain.

"Why not just jump in the river and float to where you want to go?" I ask.

"You can't get there that way," they answer.

"How do you know?" I ask.

I get no reply.

Genius is what you do without exerting a lot of effort. Michael Jordan was easeful at playing basketball. He didn't get to where he was by working harder than everyone else. He got to his level of play by doing what was easy for him to do. This does *not* mean that genius is not work. Jordan spent a lot of hours practicing. No matter how good he was, he never got past the need to practice. Still, even practice comes easily when you are practicing your genius. In short, genius defines the space where work is easy and life comes to us easily.

Exercise:
1. Of the things you did today, what was hard? Write whatever comes into your head. Don't critique it or give it second thoughts.
2. What did you do today that came easily to you? List everything; big and small.
3. If you chose to design your day tomorrow to make it as easeful as possible, what would it look like?

THE FEEDBACK KEY

We like to say that the world is giving you feedback all the time. The question is not "Are you getting feedback?" Rather, it's "Are you listening?" One great way of discovering your genius is simply to ask the people in your life for their answer to the question, "What do you think is my genius?" You will be amazed at what you learn. Go back through your old report cards and the feedback you remember from teachers, coaches, and the parents of your friends. What did they tell you about your gifts and talents? Where did they advise you *not* to go? What nicknames did they call you? Ask the people in your life today: subordinates, peers, managers (past and present), friends, children, and significant others. Is there a pattern in their answers?

Too often we guide our lives by the course prescribed by the world rather than seeking the one that fits our uniqueness. We get caught up like a surfer on a wave and struggle to navigate it without falling off the board. For instance, in the investment world, you might start your career doing research. If you succeed, you become a portfolio manager. Somewhere in between, you're also tapped to run the team, so now you're managing people as well as investments.

Though this might describe the typical notion of the ideal progression, it assumes that the higher position is built on the skills obtained in the succession of lower ones. Furthermore, it requires either that you have genius at each position, or that you do something successfully that does not engage you fully, drains you of energy, and teaches you how to compromise your greatest gifts so as to fit into the system. How much better if, rather than climbing that ladder, you seek and hold out for the place that fits you the best?

Exercise:
1. List all the feedback you have received throughout your life. Linger over this. What have others said that you do really well? What have they said that you don't do very well?
2. List what the people in your present life say is your genius. If you don't know, ask them.
3. What patterns do you see?
4. What do you conclude?
5. How can you move your life more in the direction of that which you have identified as being your genius?

MOVING INTO GENIUS

Some people are sufficiently fortunate and/or insightful to know, embrace, and follow their genius from childhood. They experience solid success, satisfaction, and peace. The majority of us understand and approve the concept of knowing and following one's genius, but need to know how to get there or how to do it.

The most important myth to dispel in this regard is that to live in your genius requires quitting your job, buying a loft, and embarking on an oil-painting career; or some other radical and disruptive change. Rarely have we strayed as far off our paths as we imagine or fear. The strength of our genius exerts such a strong influence on our lives that it unconsciously guides our choices even if we have not been paying attention. However, clarity, conviction, and commitment to live in alignment with our genius is what unleashes its full potential in our lives. There are three steps in that alignment:

Step 1: Get as clear as you can about your genius.
Step 2: Set your intention to live in your genius.
Step 3: Complete the quadrant exercise.

Step 1: Get as Clear as You Can about Your Genius

No one can peg his or her genius with absolute certainty. After all, our lives are a work of art in perpetual progress, and we don't need to have life that well defined. It is enough if we know the general direction and are open to learning about and refining that knowledge as we progress. Surely you can construct a list as long as your arm of things you are currently doing that you know are not reflective of your genius. Knowing what it is not is helpful, too.

Now, review the work you did earlier in the chapter and complete these sentences:

"To the best of my knowledge, at this point in my life, my genius is NOT _____."

"To the best of my knowledge, at this point in my life, my genius IS _____."

Simply taking this step puts you far ahead of many people who are committed to stumbling along without clarity as to what lights their fire and defines their greatness.

Step 2: Set Your Intention to Live in Your Genius

Intention is a powerful concept. Intention defines how we utilize our energy. More than merely what one has in mind to do or bring about, *intention* for our purposes includes those issues we truly care about in our lives. These issues may be far different from the ones we believe (or are told) we should care about.

For example, almost everyone who is overweight believes that losing weight is a good idea, but not everyone who is overweight has the intention to lose weight. Only when you see your overweight friend at the gym and eating salads can you know that he or she has the intention to lose weight.

The same is true of genius. Almost everyone in the investment world to whom we introduce the idea of genius sees it as powerful and potentially helpful, yet not everyone puts it to use. Those who do not almost always have some commitment other than to live in their genius. The following list notes some of the common intentions that compete with the genius intention:

- The intention to do what I am told and keep my head down.
- The intention to live for an early retirement.
- The intention to do enough to get by.
- The intention to build character by doing what is hard.
- The intention to do as little as possible.
- The intention to hate work and live for the weekends.
- The intention to complain about the firm and engage in gossip.
- The intention to "kiss up" to get ahead.
- The intention to be mediocre.
- The intention to be comfortable.

Though it might not be pleasant to admit to yourself what your current intention is in relation to your genius, doing so is extremely helpful. Intentions don't change by guilt, pressure, or shame. They don't yield to change because you come across a good idea. The best way to shift your intention is to:

- Bring your current intention to *conscious attention*.
- Accept it as *true*.
- Believe that it has *served you well* in some regard.
- Be open to the idea that a *new intention might now serve you better*.
- Live with the issue *unsettled* until you know you are ready to change.
- When you are ready, *commit* to changing your intention to live in your genius.

That is how it works with a diet, isn't it? No diet works when you aren't really committed to it. You always find ways to bend the rules until you have eroded its entire efficacy. No matter what others want you to do, or how good an idea the diet seems to be, you know you are undermining its potential benefit. Then, one day, you wake up and you have a new intention: "Today, I want to be on a diet." You feel it from the top of your head to the soles of your feet. When that intention is in place, any diet will work.

The point is to *get clear about your intention regarding your genius*. If you are not ready to know it and live committed to it, give yourself freedom to say so. If, however, your intention is to embrace your genius, you have taken Step 2.

Step 3: Complete the Quadrant Exercise

Once we intend to live in our genius, we begin to notice all the interference and competition for our time that, previously, went completely unnoticed. Genius requires becoming aware of and intentional about how you use your time. One of the best tools we have found in working with those in the investment community is the Task Quadrants. These quadrants help to concretely identify how you use and misuse your giftedness on a daily basis. First, let's examine each one.

Incompetent.   This quadrant asks two questions:

- What are you doing that almost everyone else can do better than you?
- What are you doing about which you get negative feedback?

We all know people who are committed to incompetence or mediocrity. They spend their days doing things at which they just aren't very good. Their work is plain vanilla. They don't distinguish themselves in any way. It is very difficult for someone who lives in this quadrant to survive in the kinds of firms with which we work. These people are flushed through the system quickly. There simply is no place for individuals who fill their work lives with tasks and responsibilities that are far removed from their genius. When we are brought in to coach such a misplaced hire, the task is to help him see that his true commitment is to suffering and frustration. He is bringing on failure and failure is headed his way.

Now, look at your day. What do you do in your day at which you are, at best, only mediocre? Take the time to make a list. Everything on your list is a drain on your genius, a diversion from living in a place of high energy, creativity, success, and satisfaction. Often you can identify these tasks by noticing when you procrastinate.

Shifting to genius means offloading as many of these tasks as possible to someone whose genius gifts cover that task. It might take a little creativity to do this, and you might not be able to shift everything. Still, whatever progress you make will give you a great return on investment.

Competent. This quadrant is defined by slightly different questions:

- What work do you do that others can do as well or better?
- What work do you do well, but is not totally satisfying?

Again, take the time to make a list of things you do regularly that fall into the Competent Quadrant.

If almost everything you do in your day fits into this quadrant, we suggest that you are unconsciously committed to sleepwalking, going through the motions, maintaining the status quo. Folks in this quadrant have given up on the dream of success and have settled for riding out their careers in some safe corner of the firm where they will not be noticed. They have lost sight of their tremendous gifts and the joy they could have from making their full contribution. (When Jim Ware determined that he was going to leave his steady job to found the Focus Consulting Group, one of his investment peers said, "Jim, be serious!

Only seven more years and you'll be fully vested!" In the seven years following Jim's departure, he has authored 4 books, spoken in 15 countries, and appeared many times on national television. Living in one's genius involves a wholly different set of priorities than living a safe and secure life.)

We have found that many people handle a fair number of tasks and responsibilities that fall within this quadrant. Don't be surprised if you are one of them. Realize, though, that these tasks are not within your genius. They will never lead to your wild success! They will never bring you great satisfaction and fulfillment. In fact, they are crowding your schedule and stealing the opportunity for you to spend time in more productive ways. They are weeds in the garden of your life, and it is up to you to pluck them out so that the flowers can grow unencumbered.

Which of the tasks on your "competent" list could you simply stop doing, or delegate or shift to someone else? You won't know until you try. Every success you create opens space for work that is much more useful and productive.

We say that both the Competent and Incompetent Quadrants are energy depleters. By that we mean that anyone who allocates the majority of her time to such tasks has set her sail either for failure or for simply getting by. No high achiever allows such a waste of resources. People committed to their genius perpetually keep one eye on these two quadrants and are always finding new strategies to offload the tasks therein.

We recently coached an executive of a large investment firm on the use of the quadrants. He discovered that he spent one to two hours a day wading through and answering e-mail. It certainly was not energizing for him. It also clearly fit in the Competent Quadrant: he was competent at the task, but it was not satisfying. After giving some thought to the issue, he gave the task to his administrative assistant, who excels at quickly sorting the messages and reviewing them with him twice a day. The executive thereby recovered 90 minutes each day that he now spends working in the areas of his genius.

Excellent. In this quadrant, we are finally gaining energy. Everything in this quadrant feels much more positive and useful. The questions asked in this quadrant are:

- What do you do better than just about everyone else?
- What do you do in your work that consistently gets you positive feedback?

Most people consider this to be the highest level of work. People operating in their Excellent Quadrant are succeeding and excelling, gaining recognition and standing out from the crowd.

But still there is more.

People committed to working out of the Excellent Quadrant are unconsciously committed to doing well by playing it safe. They like the feeling of success and the rewards that success brings, but they have not pulled out all the stops. This gap defines the difference between a very good player and an all-star. To some extent, people in this quadrant are still playing a game defined by someone else. They have not yet fully committed to working and living out of the guiding empowerment of their own personal genius.

What do you do that is excellent? Again, take the time to make a list. Write down whatever comes to mind. Don't let false modesty stand in the way of acknowledging what you do that is excellent. Don't offload these tasks. Know that they lie close enough to your genius that some small shift in what you are doing or how you are doing it will be enough to maximize your talent and satisfaction.

Genius. The greatest of all ways to live is in full and complete commitment to your genius. Genius asks these questions:

- What do you so love doing that it doesn't feel like work?
- What aspects of your work produce the highest ratio of positive results for time spent?

Here is a place to linger for a while. What do you do that doesn't feel like work? What work do you do that you would choose to do even if you didn't get paid for it? In other words, what do you do that provides innate satisfaction, where the greatest satisfaction is in doing the task, not in what you get in return? This concept is perhaps best understood in the world of artists and craftspersons, where monetary compensation may sometimes be lacking but the fulfillment of the work is enormous. The satisfaction is in the doing.

Operating in the Genius Quadrant means you can get really good results without having to kill yourself or turn your life inside out. You can do this easefully, playfully, and creatively. This is work that gives you energy rather than draining it, that uses and expands your creativity so you get better and better every day. Remember, everyone has such a place; such excitement and satisfaction really is available to everyone.

Write down those things you do that satisfy the criteria for using your genius gifts; that is, you do them effortlessly and experience great success with your creativity fully engaged.

PERSONAL ALIGNMENT

Although genius is available to everyone, the question is, "Are you committed to shift?" If the answer is yes, what will you do to make that shift happen? We find that the difference between successful and mediocre people is that successful people don't run across a good idea without putting it to use. If you think the ideas presented here are useful and put them to use in your life, that's evidence of your intention to be successful.

At this point, we invite you to make a shift in the way you are working and living that will bring you into closer alignment with your genius.

- Bring all your lists from the preceding exercises together and assign the tasks identified there into the four quadrants, as appropriate. Write down your best guess about your genius.
- Brainstorm and prioritize concrete plans to offload as many of your mediocre and competent tasks as possible. To the best of your ability, assign names and dates to who and when these will be assigned. Don't let your fear of letting go get in your way.
- Now, consider what changes you can make that will allow you more time and energy for your genius gifts. Can you carve out an hour to do what you do best? Can you redistribute responsibilities with your peers so that each person is doing more of what he or she does best?

- Next, write dates next to the top three to five changes you want to make. Check with yourself. Do you really want to do these things? If so, experiment with these changes. For example, one experiment is to make these changes when you are going to be out of the office or on vacation. Then keep the changes in place when you return. How does it feel? Can these changes become permanent? See how these changes work for you.
- After you have been shifting your work for a month, check in with yourself. How are you doing? How is your interest? Your energy? Do you feel more alive? Are you getting better results? Are you happier?

This is the pathway to aligning with your genius.

TEAM ALIGNMENT

Another opportunity to shift into greater alignment with your genius creates a win for others as well. In our work with investment teams to improve cooperation, efficiency, and effectiveness, we have discovered that work assignments are most often made based on title and position, not genius. Everyone has a list of responsibilities that are often distributed as follows:

- Incompetent Quadrant—some
- Competent Quadrant—many
- Excellent Quadrant—most
- Genius Quadrant—few

We see this as a tremendous waste of human capital and money. A recent survey reported that the average American worker wastes 2.5 hours per day while on the job.[2] Rather than being fully engaged in their tasks, they are finding other things to do: personal research on the Internet, chatting with friends, or shopping during lunch breaks. Much of this waste results from the assignment of work that is not interesting, challenging, and growth-producing.

We work with firms to maximize everyone's contribution and efficiency. One process change we advocate is to bring projects to the team and allow the team to distribute the work according to genius. Each team member is encouraged to take on whatever tasks lie in his or her areas of either excellence or genius. Two wonderful outcomes result from this change:

1. People are far more engaged in their work. They work more efficiently, bring more creativity to what they do, and produce a better product.
2. Staffing needs become obvious. The tasks that no one wants indicate the need to hire someone for whom these tasks lie in the genius quadrant. Rather than asking people to do things at which they are not very good, will procrastinate in doing, and will avoid, the team will be significantly strengthened by a new hire filling that void with his or her own genius.

We were working on genius with two leaders at K.G. Redding, both extremely gifted and skilled in the REIT world. One leader's genius is that he has a creative mind and finds absolute delight in solving puzzles. This gift equips him to quickly, effortlessly, and accurately understand a seller's motives and anxieties. His intuitive understanding, combined with research and financial analysis, has given Redding a huge competitive advantage. His counterpart is gifted at visualizing and building a business from conception to implementation. Together they are a dynamic duo.

They had not considered, however, how the genius of one created laborious and burdensome work streams for others. With the assistance of Focus Consulting Group, they divided their tasks to better honor their individual geniuses. Once that was done, they discovered the need to search for a new hire whose genius is to do the implementations tasks that neither leader delighted in doing.

Another genius matched pair was Gary Brinson and Jeff Diermeier, when they worked together at Brinson Partners. Gary loved the analytical, process-driven side of investing, whereas Jeff enjoyed the creative, big-picture pursuits.

CONCLUSION

Genius is a very powerful, and often overlooked, concept. Those who understand it and use it well create for themselves substantial success, satisfaction, and contentment. Those who don't use their genius find their careers taxing, anxiety-producing, wearing, and noxious. Those who live in their genius are energized by their work, creatively engaged in ways that only sharpen their skills and improve their performance. Those who don't are just hanging on waiting for retirement.

The shift to genius can be challenging. It demands courage. It requires taking ownership of your life and creating something positive. Every firm that makes this shift part of its culture, by encouraging personal growth, insight, and fluid distribution of responsibilities, will capitalize on the brightness of each person's innate potential. Waste will be dramatically reduced. Your firm will be known for the efficiency, creativity, and collaboration of its people.

SUMMARY

- Success and satisfaction are highly correlated with how well your job responsibilities and firm's culture fit your natural skills and abilities—that is, your genius.
- Your genius is indicated by those things that bring you success, that give you delight, that utilize your creativity, that you do with ease, and for which you consistently receive positive feedback.
- The steps to living in your genius are:
  Step 1: Get as clear as you can about your genius.
  Step 2: Set your intention to live in your genius.
  Step 3: Complete the quadrant exercise.
- How and where you spend your time can be categorized into four quadrants or zones: Incompetent, Competent, Excellent, and Genius.
- Teams are more efficient and effective when work assignments are made based on Excellent- or Genius-Quadrant capabilities rather than titles.

NEXT STEPS

- Determine if you are willing to identify and commit to living more fully in your genius. If you are willing, then make a personal "I commit" statement to shift into living in your Excellent and Genius zones.

- Create lists of those things mentioned in the "Keys to Finding Genius" section (success, delight, creativity, ease, and feedback). Analyze the lists and see if you can determine a pattern or underlying commonality in the five lists. Is a clear message coming through about your genius?

- Complete the quadrant exercise (Incompetent, Competent, Excellent, and Genius) and identify in which quadrant your tasks belong. Then, for one week, diligently track how much time you spend on those tasks. (This is easier than you think; most of the information is already on your Outlook calendar or PDA.) At the end of the week, tally your times and determine what percentage of your time you are spending in each quadrant. How does that ratio of time spent compare to your commitment to live in your genius?

- Introduce the quadrant exercise to your team members and ask them to complete it based on their current and past responsibilities. Ask them if they each want to debrief their quadrants with the team. (Careful: make this totally voluntary.) Compile the individual quadrants into a master "Team Quadrant" and use that as one tool when determining work assignments for your next project. When the project is completed, debrief and refine this process with the team.

- When determining the skills and cultural fit of the next new hire on your team, use the Team Quadrant document created in the previous step to identify gaps in the team. Focus your attention on skills appearing in the Incompetent and Competent zones of the current team members. If those are skills needed by the team, focus on looking for candidates who culturally fit the team and have a genius in those gap skills.

◆

CHAPTER 9

Appreciation
Shifting from Entitlement

Jim Dethmer

Expectations are premeditated resentments.
—Saying from Alcoholics Anonymous program

ppreciation is a choice. Like all the best behaviors of high-performing investment firms, appreciation is something the individual controls. At any moment, we can make a conscious choice to shift our focus and behaviors to appreciation.

What do we mean when we say *appreciation*? It's more than the childhood lesson of saying "thank you" or sending flowers to our assistants on a designated day of the year. First, let's start with what appreciation is not.

ENTITLEMENT

We've been told that human beings are unique among all living things in that they have the ability to anticipate and imagine what the future might hold. Instinctual animals have the ability to prepare for the future, but they do so not by worrying about or anticipating the future, but rather by living in the moment in such a way that, for example, when winter comes they have collected enough nuts to last until spring.

This ability to anticipate the future is not a bad thing. In fact, there are many good aspects to it. If left unchecked, though, it can create a vicious cycle, which goes like this.

Imagine for a moment that you are having a hard day at the office. Neither the markets nor your clients are cooperating, and your team-mates seem more like enemy combatants than fellow soldiers in the fight. Your one bright spot is that you know when the day is over, you're going to meet your spouse for a 7:30 PM dinner at your favorite restaurant. By 5:30, you find yourself focusing on the restaurant like a vision of an oasis in the desert of this dreadful day. In particular, you can see yourself sitting down to an ice-cold Grey Goose martini with two blue-cheese-stuffed olives, followed by a medium-rare filet with a twice-baked potato, and topping off the feast with the best blueberry cheesecake ever made. You don't eat dessert often, but tonight will be an exception—you deserve it!

By the time you arrive at the restaurant, your anticipation has shifted to expectation. Anticipation is sourced in excitement (and sometimes fear). You were excited about ending the day in the perfect place, with the perfect person, eating the perfect meal, and finishing with the perfect dessert. Expectation has a different tone: It is more narrow and focused than anticipation. It arises more from the region of anger and the desire to control.

Things haven't gone your way today and, damn it, you expect your favorite restaurant to save the day. It had *better* save the day. (It always does.)

At this point the expectation is about to become entitlement. You arrive at the restaurant to find that your table is not ready and won't be for another 20 minutes. A bit indignant, you mention to the host that you had reservations for 7:30. He acknowledges the slip and apologizes, but says there is nothing he can do.

Next, the bartender regretfully informs you that they're out of Grey Goose. A little disappointed, you settle for Ketel One, but you're not happy about it, especially since the guy at the end of the bar just ate the last two blue-cheese-stuffed olives.

Once at the table, your waiter describes some wonderful specials, but you don't listen because you are laser-focused on the filet and the twice-baked potato. When you finally get the steak, it's overcooked, but you're too hungry to wait for another to be prepared.

Finally, your entitlement breaks full out when you are informed that the last piece of blueberry cheesecake was just served to another table.

Entitlement goes beyond "I'm anticipating it" or "I want it" or "I expect it." Entitlement is "I deserve it. I have a right to it. It's mine." Entitlement is the opposite of appreciation. When we live in entitlement, we spend a lot of time complaining, either outwardly or inwardly. Depending on personality type, some of us are comfortable complaining outwardly; others rarely utter an audible word of complaint, but fill our internal dialogue (those conversations we hold in our minds) with complaint and criticism. We think the reason there is so little genuine appreciation in the investment business is that most of us choose the easier path of entitlement (see Figure 9.1).

A good way to discover your subtle entitlements is to be honest about what angers or frustrates you. Just to prime the pump, stop right now and make a list of things you believe you are entitled to. To get started, use this formulation to question yourself:

"When I don't get _____, I get angry (or frustrated)."

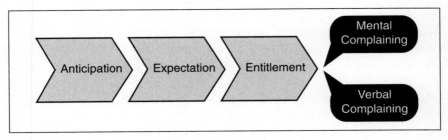

FIGURE 9.1 Entitlement.

For example:

> "When I don't get treated with respect, I get angry."
> "When I don't get included in the decision-making process at work, I get upset."
> "When I don't receive the bonus I wanted, I get frustrated."
> "When I don't get the daily performance report by 7:00 AM, I get irritated."
> "When I don't immediately get my phone messages, I get angry."
> "When I get incorrect pricing information, I get frustrated."

Keep the exercise going by completing the following sentences. If you get stuck, return to what angers or irritates you in the following contexts.

> At work, I'm entitled to _____.
> At home, I'm entitled to _____.
> With my kids, I'm entitled to _____.
> When I travel, I'm entitled to _____.
> When I'm driving, I'm entitled to _____.

If you are honest and self-aware as you go through this exercise, you'll discover that you have developed many conscious and unconscious entitlements. When you feel you are entitled to something, there is no room for appreciation.

WHAT IS APPRECIATION?

There are two definitions of *appreciation* that we find particularly helpful in this discussion. The first is "to be sensitively aware." When I appreciate something, I am sensitively aware of it. I pay attention and my attention has a certain quality to it. I pay attention with a quality of noticing or seeing as if for the first time, being pleasantly surprised by what I might see or discover. This form of appreciation can be experienced when you visit an art gallery or listen to a symphony or watch a favorite athlete perform. Though you might have seen the Monet before, you are paying attention with the possibility of seeing something new or seeing something old in a new way. Though you have heard Mozart before, you go to the symphony being willing to be surprised and delighted. You've watched Tiger Woods swing a golf club before. This time, though, you pay attention and notice how much shoulder turn he gets while not turning his hips much at all and you appreciate what he can do (and you can't).

To appreciate is to be sensitively aware. To pay attention. To see something or someone with fresh eyes. Recently, we were working with the senior management team of a large mutual fund on the power of appreciation. We went to the company dining room for lunch and, when we returned, the senior portfolio manager's assistant immediately handed me a message that she had taken for me from one of the team members who was not in the office that day. In addition to being timely, the message contained all the information I needed about the topic of the call. I said to her, "I really appreciate you for not only taking messages for me, but for being so thorough and timely." Her reaction told me that she was not used to people verbally appreciating her efforts on a casual or daily basis.

As we resumed the afternoon session, I relayed this story to the senior management team. The senior portfolio manager spoke up for the team and said, "But that's her job. I don't get it?" They had stopped paying attention and being sensitively aware of the assistant's diligence and dedication. They were no longer surprised or delighted by what she did. They had seen it all before. I told them, "If you're willing, you could actually change the way you see her. You could bring a new quality of attention to your relationship and with it a freshness of appreciation."

They were willing. How you perceive something or someone is a *choice*.

Often people are not paying attention with the intention of noticing something they have not seen or experienced about a person or a situation. Rather, their attention has a quality of "Ho-hum, I've seen that a million times before" or "Gotcha." Sometimes, they're looking for what someone isn't doing right or how another person is messing up. (*Note:* Most investment professionals are "Rationalists" in the Myers-Briggs personality trait schema. Rationalists have a genius for analyzing and finding shortcomings. Beware when they focus this talent on colleagues and staff!)

The second definition of *appreciation* is "to effortlessly grow in value." Investment people understand this definition better than most, though they might question whether any investment "effortlessly" grows in value. Think for a moment about a house, though. As I write this chapter, I'm sitting on the deck of our home in northern Michigan. This is my favorite place in the world to be during the summer months. As I sit here writing, I don't hear the house grunting or groaning. It is not putting forth any sort of effort, in any way, yet it is steadily and rapidly growing in value.

When we coach people on this subject of appreciation, we often ask them if they would be willing to have people and things in their lives grow in value in their minds and hearts, and for this growth to be effortless. Before you read any further, answer these questions for yourself.

- Would you be willing to have people you work with become more valuable to you?
- Would you be willing to have your firm as a whole and your unique job become more valuable to you?
- Would you be willing to have issues, concerns, and problems in your life actually start to become valuable to you?
- Would you be willing to have all this value accrue without a lot of effort?

If your answer to these questions is yes, you are on the road to living a life of appreciation.

To summarize our definition, to *appreciate* people or things is to pay attention to them in such a way that they effortlessly grow in value.

TWO CIRCLES OF LIFE

In the circle of entitlement, we begin by having a way we want things to be (see Figure 9.2). In and of itself, this preference for how we want things to be is not a bad thing; in fact, it can be the first step in creating a vision for a life or a firm. Within the circle of entitlement, though, we start to tighten our grip on the way we want things to be. Our desire begins to turn into an expectation. We stop seeing the way we want things to be as a *possibility* and start seeing it as the way things *ought* to be. When we can see things that we want as a possibility or an option, we can remain open and curious to other options and possibilities; we are still taking life as it

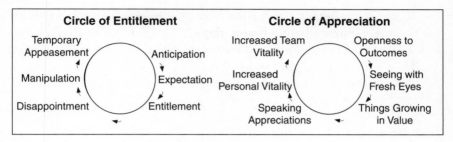

FIGURE 9.2 Circles of life.

comes to us. When we start to see what we want as being the way things "ought to be," though, we are limiting and constricting what life has to offer and teach us. We've made a transition from what we *want* to what we *expect*.

It's one thing if I want my 13-year-old daughter Hilary to love playing tennis. I could want this because I think it would be fun to play tennis with her, and because I love tennis and think it would be great if she did, too. I could want this because I think tennis is a great sport for life that she could enjoy for many years. I could want this because I think it's a great way for her to build self-confidence, or to make friends, or to earn a scholarship to college. I could want it for all kinds of reasons.

When I start tightening my grip on my desire, it becomes an expectation. I *expect* her to love tennis. I love tennis, so, of course, she'll love tennis. The rest of our family all plays tennis, so she'll play tennis. Tennis is a big part of our summers in Michigan, so tennis should be a big part of her life. From this perspective, I start to limit what life has to offer to me, to Hilary, and to the family. I start to see only what I want to see. Now, if Hilary has a natural love for tennis, there will be no overt conflict. She is cooperating with my expectation. If she doesn't love tennis, though, drama is just over the horizon.

This type of situation occurs repeatedly in investment firms. We were coaching an officer in the operations area of an institutional money manager. On our first day of coaching, the officer walked in and said, "I'm so upset. My best accounting manager just told me she's leaving."

Sensing a great coaching opportunity, we probed a bit about the situation.

"I only wanted her to be the best she can be. I encouraged her to get her CFA designation like I did—it makes a huge difference when you look at all the opportunities it would open up for her."

We asked, "So, what happened?"

"Well, I kept at her for a couple of years and she finally came around and sat for Level I in June."

"And . . . "

"She passed. I knew she would."

"But . . . "

"She said she didn't want to do it for two more years and, since that's what I expected, she got a job where she can focus on what she loves doing. She just doesn't see how great she could be if only . . . "—if only the accounting manager would fit herself into the officer's expectation of what she *should* be doing. This single-minded expectation cost the officer a star employee because the officer couldn't see beyond that expectation.

If I hold my wants loosely and am open to what life has to offer, I might see that my daughter Hilary likes tennis fine, but what she really loves is wakeboarding or kayaking. Life has brought me a daughter who is more at home on the water than on the court.

If our operations officer had held her wants loosely, she might have seen that her accounting manager really loved accounting—and that's it. The accounting manager wasn't interested in a career path that would take her away from accounting, and did not have any interest in pursuing the CFA. (Jamie Ziegler, the marketing director for the Focus Consulting Group, also passed CFA level I, then realized that her real genius was branding, promotion, and marketing, not company analysis. She has thrived in the marketing world.)

If I don't hold my wants loosely—if I let them slip into becoming expectations and entitlements—the following often occurs. When Hilary comes home from tennis lessons and isn't excited, I'll try to figure out how to get her excited. Maybe she needs more lessons. Maybe she needs more competition. Maybe I should play tennis with her every night. Maybe she needs a talking-to or an attitude adjustment. Maybe she needs me to convince her that she is wrong to think the way she does about tennis. I could do this by complaining, by cajoling, or by becoming caustic or critical. After all, I'm entitled to have a daughter who loves tennis, right?

For a time it might work. If I crank up the pressure high enough, I might be able to get Hilary to go along with my program, like the operations officer did with her accounting manager. Eventually, though, Hilary will follow her own program rather than mine, just as the accounting manager did when she quit to get away from the demands of her officer's expectations.

When we live in the entitlement circle, we regularly try to get people in our lives to be the way we want them to be. We do this nicely, if nicely works; if it doesn't, we all have our particular forms of ratcheting up the pressure. Often people will comply for a while, but such compliance is usually short-lived, and when they drift back to not doing what we want/expect/think we're entitled to, the vicious cycle starts all over again. That's why people in this circle live lives characterized by tension, conflict, drama, and disappointment.

What's the other option?

The second circle is the circle of appreciation. In the circle of appreciation, I begin by having the intention to be pleasantly surprised by what life offers me. Even though I might have wants and desires, I am much more interested in playing with what life brings me. My life is more like a great jazz ensemble, improvising rather than playing strictly from sheet music I have composed to dictate every note the band should play.

From this posture of openness, I have the intention of seeing situations, people, problems, and possibilities with fresh eyes and of having a dynamic perspective on all of it so that all these things grow in value effortlessly. Going back to our operations officer, instead of looking at her accounting manager with eyes for what that person was missing (for example, a CFA designation), she would have been open to seeing what the accounting manager was already contributing to the organization, valuing those contributions, and appreciating the manager for bringing that talent to the team every day. Unfortunately for the officer, she didn't do that until she read the manager's resignation letter.

I try not to have expectations about the way people and situations ought to be. I try not to exert the death grip of entitlement on how life should come to me. My goal is to be open, curious, and perceptive, open to what life is tossing my way. For the operations officer in our example, the combination of the resignation letter and our appreciation coaching opened her up to make a commitment to eliminate expectations of people and situations. It wasn't easy for her, an over-planning perfectionist, but she made a commitment and shifted. On one of our follow-up visits, she said she had been shocked by what she had realized over the last couple of weeks. She was becoming consciously aware and appreciative of so many things that she had previously expected and taken for granted.

As I wrote this, I had a chance to apply what I'm talking about. I was sitting at the LaGuardia airport waiting for a flight back to Michigan. That night, my extended family was gathering for dinner to celebrate my stepson's engagement. His fiancée and her family were there as well, and a good time was had by all—but I wasn't there.

Our team had been working with the analysts at Sanford Bernstein and I left early to catch a 2:00 PM flight back to Michigan. What life tossed my way was a traffic accident on the Grand Central Parkway. I could feel my anticipation for a fun dinner growing as my perspective constricted. As I sat in traffic, I subtly shifted from anticipation to expectation, and by the time I got to the airline ticket counter, I was in full-blown entitlement. My e-ticket wouldn't print because it said I was too close to the departure time. Believing I was entitled to get on the flight, I rather pushily made my way to the front of the ticket-agent line and asked the agent to print my boarding pass. She told me that I had missed the deadline by two minutes and that I wouldn't be able to board the flight. I assured her that if she would just print the ticket, I would make it through security and to the flight because I had no bags to check. She said she "couldn't" oblige me because of company rules.

By then, I was in full-fledged entitlement meltdown: complaining, cajoling, coming up with all kinds of reasons why what I wanted had to be what life gave me. I was angry and sad. I called my wife to tell her I wouldn't make it home for the party. Then I got on a flight that wouldn't get me home until after midnight . . . if it got there at all, as thunderstorms were headed toward New York.

But then I shifted.

It took about 90 minutes, but I made the choice to shift from entitlement to appreciation; from expectation to openness; from trying to force my will on the universe to playing a jazz riff with what was coming my way. (Another popular saying in 12-step programs is: "Learn to live life on life's terms.")

After I acknowledged my feelings of anger and sadness, I spent some time deep breathing and walking. On the walk, I asked myself, "Do I want to shift or stay in entitlement?"

I decided I wanted to shift.

My first shift-move was to recommit to living in appreciation, recommit to taking responsibility for what I had created, and try openly get all the learnings. I then started asking "wonder" questions, such as, "I wonder what I could do for the next few hours that would allow this to be a fun learning experience?" "I wonder how I could have a really good time here in New York?" These wonderings and others began to shift me. I can honestly say that I eventually opened to seeing this situation with fresh eyes and to having it effortlessly grow in value based on the choices I made in answer to those questions. I became fully committed to being alive right where I was.

Notice that everything we've talked about so far regarding the circle of appreciation takes place internally. It's a choice about how we want to see the world. The next step in the circle moves the inward commitment of fresh eyes and effortless increase in value to an outward experience of how we speak to and treat others.

From this place of appreciation, we can regularly make a choice to speak our appreciations to the people in our lives. This is a simple act with profound consequences. The act is so simple because all it involves is saying to someone, "I appreciate you for . . . ." That's it. The only criteria are that the appreciation be sincere and not intended to get a response of any kind. False appreciation is actually *flattery*. Appreciation designed to get a response is *praise*. Appreciation is neither of these. It is simply noticing something about someone that you genuinely appreciate and expressing it because it is natural to express appreciation. The value of appreciating is primarily for the appreciator, though it will often have a positive effect on the one being appreciated as well.

Which circle do you want to live in? It's a choice. Our belief is that most of the world lives in the circle of complaint and entitlement and that few choose the circle of appreciation. The best investment teams choose the circle of appreciation.

APPRECIATION AND TEAMS

John Gottman, PhD, is one of the leading experts on marriage in the world. Gottman is possibly most famous for his ability to predict the outcome of a relationship. After watching a couple have a 60-minute conversation about a meaningful, but not necessarily controversial, topic, Gottman can predict with 95% accuracy whether the couple will still be married 15 years from now. He can watch a 15-minute video and predict with 90% accuracy whether they will stay together. He does this by paying detailed attention to the presence of certain predictors. He has found a very high correlation between the presence of defensiveness, blame, contempt, and stonewalling and the health of a marriage. From Gottman's perspective as a research scientist, he has reached a powerful conclusion:

> Marriages that have a 5:1 ratio of positive to negative communication have a good probability of succeeding. Relationships that have only a 1:1 ratio will usually fail.[1]

That's sobering stuff: A 1:1 ratio of positive interactions to negative interactions is a high predictor of relational failure! Can this really be so?

Further validation of this conclusion comes from the world of professional sports. When we attended a dinner with Phil Jackson, the successful basketball coach of the Los Angeles Lakers and Chicago Bulls, Phil told us that his coaching philosophy was to give five compliments for every one criticism. In fact, a cardinal principle of the Positive Coaching Alliance, for which Phil is the national spokesperson, is to teach coaches at all levels the value of a ratio of five positive interactions for every one that is constructively critical.

The same is true in the investment world. A common attribute of the highest-performing teams with sustainable success is that their positive interactions predominate over neutral-to-negative interactions.

APPRECIATION AND CANDOR

We cannot stress enough that what we are talking about here is not some Pollyanna-ish, sunny-side-of-the-street, denial-of-reality way of being. In fact, our view is just the opposite. We believe in open, honest, truthful, full-out conversations as well as a steady dose of appreciation.

- If there is an issue, address it.
- If there is a problem, face it.
- If there is a situation, confront it.

And choose to pay attention to each other with sensitivity, while having the intention of having every relationship grow in value. If you are not candid, your appreciation will be hollow, and if you are not appreciative, your candor will become toxic.

WHY DO WE RESIST APPRECIATION?

One of the exercises we take teams through when we are teaching them the value of appreciation is to ask them to complete the following sentences:

- "If I showered people around me with genuine appreciation, I would be afraid that . . . "
- "If I was showered with genuine appreciation, I would be afraid that . . . "

Before we go any further, ask yourself the same two questions. Your answers will reveal your beliefs about appreciation. If you're like many of the investment professionals we work with, you probably believe that if you showered people with genuine appreciation,

- They would stop performing at their best.
- They would come to expect it.
- They would want more money.
- They would not believe you and think that you are trying to manipulate them.
- They would lose their edge.

You probably have similar beliefs about what would happen if people gave you lots of appreciation. Our work with investment professionals tells us that the biggest reaction you would have to people who expressed appreciation for you would be mistrust. You wouldn't believe that they were sincere, or you'd think they wanted something from you.

HARDER TO RECEIVE THAN TO GIVE

From working with investment professionals now for many years, we at Focus Consulting have come to a firm conclusion: As hard as it is for investment professionals to give appreciation (and it is *very* hard), it is even more difficult for them to receive appreciation.

When we meet with teams, we often take them through the "Appreciation Toss" exercise to give them a taste of what appreciation can do for their team and themselves.

Exercise: Everyone is asked to take a few minutes and think about the other people on the team. As they think about an individual, we ask them to mentally identify something they appreciate, really appreciate, about that individual team member. It doesn't have to be something big, but it does have to be something real. They don't have to think of something they appreciate about everyone, as this would probably force something that was not authentic. Once they have a few things they appreciate, we begin the exercise.

Some brave soul begins by addressing another member of the team. We ask the speaker to talk directly to the team member he or she is addressing and to look at that person when he or she talks. It might sound something like this:

"Bob, I appreciate you for the work you did on creating the model we use for fixed-income credit scoring." Simple, clear, direct, and genuine.

Bob is then asked to simply say, "Thank you."

This sounds easy, but it usually isn't easy for the participants. Often people are so uncomfortable about receiving appreciation that they deflect it by joking or saying something to the effect of "It was nothing," or "It really wasn't that good," or "Mary did most of the work." (Craig Pho, Director of Research at Burgundy Asset Management in Toronto, was so uncomfortable receiving positive feedback that he asked if his team could only give him the negative!) We've heard dozens of deflections. Most people need help to simply say "thank you." We call this the ability to "let the appreciation land." So often we don't let feedback of any kind really land. We deflect it on the way in.

It seems especially difficult for people in our industry to let appreciation land. One simple tool we've taught is to take one breath before you say anything. This breath often creates an opening for the feedback to land.

After Bob receives the appreciation tossed his way with a simple "thank you," we invite him to address someone else on the team and toss an appreciation to that person: "Joan, I appreciate you staying late last week to get me that industry analysis I needed for the investment committee meeting."

Although receiving the appreciation appears to be physically painful for Joan, she heeds the point of the exercise, takes a breath, and says, "Thank you."

It's always fascinating for us to watch this exercise unfold. Often it starts awkwardly, with everyone feeling and acting very self-conscious. After a few minutes, though, the group usually shifts. They enter into a state of giving and receiving appreciation. (One burly leader was so overcome by the appreciation that his team showered on him that he teared up and couldn't speak.) Then time seems to fly by and the spirit of the room seems to change.

THE VOICE OF THE INNER CRITIC

There are probably many reasons why investment people have a hard time letting appreciation land, but we're convinced that one of them is the presence of an inner critic. The *inner critic* is that voice that's constantly speaking in your head, saying things like:

- You could have done a better job writing that paragraph.
- You should call Dan Jones since he called last Friday.
- You're not doing a good enough job on your analysis of free cash flow.

- Your tie looks stupid with that suit.
- It wasn't smart to say that in this meeting.

Psychologists estimate that people have as many as 50,000 thoughts a day. Of those 50,000, what percentage of yours are self-critical? Our sense is that because you are in the investment business, you have a disproportionately high number of critical thoughts. After all, your ability to think critically is part of what makes you good at what you do. As we coach investment leaders, we discover that, at first, they are unaware of the constant presence of the inner critic. Once they become aware of it, they have a hard time turning off the voice.

The presence of an overactive inner critic is, we think, one of the reasons people in this business have a hard time receiving appreciation. The external appreciative message is so contradictory to the constant internal message of the critic that the external message is often rejected. Interestingly, we have discovered that the people with the biggest egos or the most arrogant personas often have the harshest inner critics. Their egotism and arrogance are compensation for how small they feel on the inside, because of the constant chiding of their inner critics. One key to being a great leader in the long term is learning to manage your inner critic.

One strategy for dealing with the inner critic is to make a choice to live in a state of appreciation. Another strategy we offer for dealing with your inner critic is to type up a list of 100 things you appreciate about yourself. (This is often one of the most difficult assignments we give people we coach.) Remember, the only criteria are that you have to be genuine and that you have to let the self-appreciation land. Once you have created the list, copy it into your PDA and read it once a week.

COMMITTING TO APPRECIATION

Like every other behavior that characterizes high-performing investment teams, we believe that the first step in appreciation is to get clear about your commitment. What is your current commitment to appreciation? If you're like a lot of people we deal with, it might be something like this:

- I am committed to giving appreciation once a year in performance reviews.
- I am committed to giving appreciation in the form of bonuses and not words.
- I am committed to giving appreciation in the form of a simple "thank you."
- I am committed to keeping people fearful because they perform better that way.
- I am committed to never appreciating myself for what I do because I could always do a better job.
- I am committed to not opening myself up to my co-workers by expressing appreciation.

Remember that the key to commitment is to first be honest about what you are currently committed to doing. This is evidenced by the results you are getting in your life right now. Once you get conscious and clear about your current commitments, you are ready to consider adopting a new commitment. You might consider a new commitment to appreciation that sounds something like this:

- I commit to living in a state of appreciation of myself and others and to speaking that appreciation in creative ways.
- I commit to a positive shift in my ability to give and receive appreciation.
- I commit to leading and building a culture of appreciation in our firm.

If you are committed to increasing the amount of appreciation in your life, we suggest that you do the following exercises, which have been adapted from a tool used at the Hendricks Institute.

Exercise: 30 Days of Appreciation in the Workplace

Step 1: Don't tell people that you are doing this exercise. Just do the exercise and examine the results.

Step 2: For each day, read the statement and complete the appreciation, making sure that it is heartfelt and genuine. Say it out loud to yourself before sharing it with the recipient. How does it feel? Note that you can choose a different recipient each day and that you can use the same recipient more than once.

Step 3: Ideally, approach the appreciation recipient face-to-face. If a face-to-face meeting is not possible, a real-time conversation on the telephone is the next best option. No cheating and deliberately calling after hours when you know you'll get voice mail, unless it's unavoidable. The last resort, and least preferable delivery mechanism, is e-mail.

Step 4: At the end of the 30 days, how do you feel? Is appreciation coming more easily to you? What changes have occurred in your relationship with your teammates? Are you committed to remaining in appreciation from now on?

Daily Appreciation Statements

Day 1: I appreciate you for the contribution you make to [*company name*] by _____.

Day 2: I appreciate you for the expertise you have in _____.

Day 3: I appreciate you for your leadership, as evidenced by the way you _____.

Day 4: One thing I've learned from you that I appreciate you for is _____.

Day 5: Something I really appreciate that you do without drawing attention to it is _____.

Day 6: [Today, appreciate something about your co-worker verbally to another person.] One thing I really appreciate about _____ is _____.

Day 7: One thing I appreciate about you that I have learned from you is _____.

Day 8: One thing I appreciate about the way you deal with the people who work for you is _____.

Day 9: One thing I appreciate about you that I've sometimes taken for granted is _____.

Day 10: Something about the way you see the world that I appreciate is _____.

Day 11: I appreciate the value you place on _____.

Day 12: One thing I appreciate about your mind is _____.

Day 13: I appreciate that your creativity has generated _____.

Day 14: I appreciate how much you've taught me about _____.

Day 15: One thing I appreciate about how you treat your customers is _____.

Day 16: [Today, send an e-mail or call your co-worker's boss and tell him or her one thing you appreciate about your co-worker.]

Day 17: One way in which you've grown that I appreciate is _____.

Day 18: One thing about the way you handle adversity that I appreciate is _____.

Day 19: One thing I appreciate about you that isn't related to you as a businessperson is _____.

Day 20: I appreciate you for the way you handled _____ [think of a specific situation and how your co-worker dealt with it].

Day 21: I appreciate you for going above and beyond the call of duty when you _____.

Day 22: I appreciate you for the emphasis you place on _____.

Day 23: I appreciate you for your honesty and frankness when you _____.

Day 24: I appreciate you for respecting confidentiality when you _____.

Day 25: One thing I appreciate about your humor is _____.

Day 26: One thing I appreciate about your persistence is _____.

Day 27: I appreciate you for your kindness when you
_____.

Day 28: One thing I appreciate about your convictions is
_____.

Day 29: I appreciate you for your commitment to developing people when you _____.

Day 30: I appreciate you for driving results, as evidenced in
_____.

APPRECIATION IS CONTAGIOUS

Be prepared: This stuff is contagious. One of our colleagues, Fran Skinner, decided to play the "Appreciation Toss" game with her two school-aged boys. She chose this as a distraction technique during a particularly long car ride. To her surprise, not only did the boys get into the game and come up with the most amazing appreciation comments, but they begged to play it on future occasions! Our experience is that, once introduced to a life of appreciation, people in your firm, like Fran's boys, will be saying, "Hey, can we play that appreciation game?"

For those of you who are intrigued by this notion of appreciation, we also offer "31 Days of Appreciation" for partners/spouses and a separate one for parents/children. Please contact us through our web site (*www.focusCgroup.com*) and we'll be happy to send these to you at no charge.

SUMMARY

- We have a choice to live in either appreciation or entitlement.
- Without conscious guidance, anticipation can lead to expectation and entitlement.
- Entitlement leads to negative outcomes such as anger and frustration, which can negatively affect relationships, teams, and organizations.

- Research has shown that in healthy relationships, there is at least a 5:1 ratio of appreciation and positive comments compared to negative-to-neutral comments.
- True appreciation is candid and sincere.
- Investment professionals need to be consciously aware of and manage their inner critics if they are truly to receive appreciation.

NEXT STEPS

- Determine if you want to shift from living in entitlement to living in appreciation. If you do, then make your personal commitment.
- Complete the exercise in this chapter in which you list what frustrates or angers you, and what you believe you are entitled to in the various aspects of your life. Choose two or three of the things you believe you are entitled to and ask yourself if you're willing to shift out of that entitlement into appreciation. Make a conscious effort to steer away from that entitlement for those items for one week. What do you notice?
- Choose one person on your team. For one week, make a conscious effort to see with "fresh eyes" that person and what he or she does. Appreciate that person and his or her contributions as if you were seeing them for the first time. Verbalize your appreciation throughout the week, as appropriate. At the end of the week, what observations can you make?
- Complete the "30 Days of Appreciation" exercise at work. How is your appreciation received by your teammates? How do you feel giving it? What changes do you notice at the end of the 30 days?
- For one week, without doing anything differently than you normally do, measure your ratio of positive/appreciative comments versus negative/neutral comments to your individual team members. If the ratio is less than 5:1, are you open to shifting and improving that ratio? If so, make that shift a goal.
- At your next staff meeting, go through the "Appreciation Toss" exercise with your team members. Watch for deflection and

encourage everyone to let the appreciation land with a simple "thank you."

- Choose someone with whom you have been frustrated lately, and make a list of 30 things you appreciate about that person. When you've completed the list, can you shift to genuine appreciation of that person? If so, what do you notice about your interactions going forward?

◆

CHAPTER 10

Fit
Investment Personalities and the Seven Behaviors

Jim Ware

Self-evaluation is not a strength for anyone in this business.
—Ed Jannotta, Chairman, William Blair & Co.

Certain of the seven behaviors discussed in this book come easier depending on one's personality type. Those of you who have read either of my two earlier books—*The Psychology of Money*[1] or *Investment Leadership*[2]—know that we at the Focus Consulting Group often use the Myers-Briggs personality assessment (formally known as the Myers-Briggs Type Indicator, or MBTI) in our work with investment firms. We can now predict with high accuracy the personality makeup of a money management team. As you might guess, the personalities of investment professionals are significantly different from those of other professional groups, such as firefighters, hospital workers, teachers, actuaries, craftspersons, or top athletes. These differences go a long way toward explaining which of the seven behaviors will come naturally to a particular group and which will be difficult—that is, contrary to their natural behavior. Each personality type has its strengths and weaknesses, and investment teams are no exception.

First, let's review the Myers-Briggs assessment tool. The MBTI, which is based on Carl Jung's ideas about psychological type, was designed to measure the way a brain is hard-wired. In other words, it measures the way we prefer to use our brains. A good analogy for this brain preference is handedness; that is, one's innate preference for using the left or the right hand. When asked to sign a document, none of us stops to think, "Gee, which hand will I use?" Rather, we simply pick up the pen and sign—with the preferred hand. If we had to use the nondominant hand, we would find the task awkward and difficult, and the result (the signature) would be barely legible.

The brain works in the same way. From birth, we are naturally predisposed ("wired") to do some thinking naturally and easily and other thinking with greater difficulty. Note that with practice, we can develop good, balanced skills in many areas. (Michael Jordan trained himself to be equally skillful handling a basketball with his left or right hand.) It's just that some areas require more effort, and more *conscious* effort. In *The Psychology of Money*, I showed that the top investors—Warren Buffett, Peter Lynch, and George Soros—have mastered the use of both sides of the brain, which allows them to be master investors. Other investment legends, like Gary Brinson, used a different strategy of teaming up with opposite personality types to augment their individual talents. (Brinson paired with Jeff Diermeier, creating a powerful and well-rounded intellectual arsenal.)

The MBTI measures one's preferences for four aspects of thinking:

1. Where we place attention: externally or internally.
2. How we process and analyze data: sensing or intuitive.
3. How we make decisions: thinking decisions or feeling decisions.
4. How we choose to organize our time and things: organized or flexible.

Table 10.1 describes each of these pairs.

EXTROVERSION VERSUS INTROVERSION: "OUT THERE" VERSUS "IN HERE"

Most asset managers are introverts: about 60 percent, as opposed to only 25 percent of the public at large. This is no surprise. Introverts love to read and think and then, after a break, to read and think some more! Introverts enjoy going deeply into a subject, whereas extroverts are quite

TABLE 10.1   Myers-Briggs Preferences

Extroversion (E)	Introversion (I)
• Focus is outside: people, places, things • Tends to "do–think–do" • Prefers verbal to written communication	• Focus is inside: ideas and feelings • Tends to "think–do–think" • Prefers written to verbal communication
Sensing (S)	**Intuiting (N)**
• Linear thinking • Practical; likes details • Step-by-step approach	• Creative thinking • Theoretical; likes big picture • Jumps from idea to idea
Thinking (T)	**Feeling (F)**
• Objective decision making • Tough-minded • Competitive • Goes for truth and clarity	• Subjective decision making (based on personal values) • Tender-hearted • Cooperative • Goes for warmth and kindness
Judging (J)	**Perceiving (P)**
• Organized • Decisive • Planful	• Flexible • Open to new options • Goes with the flow

happy moving from one topic to another. (Studies with infants have shown that the extroverted infants will happily play with one toy after another, whereas the introverted children stick with one favorite toy. In short, one likes variety, the other depth.)

Peter Lynch is a great example of an extrovert. He traveled 100,000 miles per year, visiting 30 to 40 managements per month, and when he wasn't traveling he used a three-minute egg timer on telephone conversations with brokers. (They learned quickly to get to the point!) Lynch was fanatical about collecting all the data he could get his hands on. He is famous for his stories about walking through the malls to discover the next great investment idea: The Gap, The Limited, and so on. From an investment team perspective, it's useful to understand the differing deep beliefs about market success for the extrovert versus the introvert:

Extrovert: "I'll win in the markets if I can get enough data and kick enough tires."

Introvert: "I'll win in the markets if I can close my door and think carefully."

Needless to say, we've seen many live examples of these two belief systems colliding. An extroverted research director was driving his intro-verted team crazy trying to get them all in a room to talk about stocks. They wanted peace and quiet; some of them actually thought this direc-tor was trying to ruin their careers! Surfacing and discussing their differ-ences allowed them to reach a reasonable compromise.

SENSING VERSUS INTUITING: BOTTOM-UP OR TOP-DOWN?

Sensors tend to be very practical people who take comfort in collecting facts. They rely on their senses: what they can touch, taste, hear, feel, and see. Seeing is believing—and that, of course, is where the terms *sensing* and *Sensor* come from. People with a preference for intuition are wired differently. They take comfort in theorizing. Data and facts are fine (maybe a little boring, actually), but the real fun lies in taking informa-tion and creating a new theory or paradigm. As mentioned earlier in this book, several leaders we work with—Kim Redding and Michael Sapir—are so intuitive that they sometimes frustrate their Sensor staff members. Why? Because Sensing types want to know how you reached your con-clusion; how did you get from A to Z? What were the steps? More often than not, Redding and Sapir cannot tell you how they reached an answer. They just know it's right. They excel at seeing the big picture and at put-ting together seemingly unrelated facts. That is their genius quality.

One story in particular highlights the basic difference between these preferences. Two men are on their knees laying bricks. You ask the first one what he is making and he responds, "I'm building a huge cathedral in which to worship God and give thanks for this wondrous universe." Whoa—there's a big thought. You approach the second man, who is doing exactly the same thing, and ask the same question, "What are you making?"

This fellow, a practical, down-to-earth Sensor, interprets the question totally differently and responds, "$17.50 an hour."

Same question, same job, different answers based on their preferences.

From an investment perspective, Sensors and Intuitors have very different beliefs about what wins in the marketplace:

Sensor: "I'll win by hard work and careful scrutiny of all the data."
Intuitor: "I'll win by seeing things differently, getting a creative insight."

A classic Sensor is short-seller James Chanos. When I first started in the business in the early 1980s, Chanos was the lone wolf crying "bogus" at the success of Baldwin United. Seasoned Wall Street analysts were pulling Chanos aside and warning the young analyst, "Pipe down, this will ruin your career. You'll be viewed as a crackpot." But the young Chanos had done his homework and pored through all the footnotes of the financial statements, so he could show that Baldwin United was creating results with smoke and mirrors. Eventually, he was proven right. The stock collapsed and Chanos's fame as a short-seller began to grow.

Years later, as Enron's stock price was still rocketing upward, guess who first shouted "bogus"? Right: James Chanos, even though the media used the same phrase to describe his research approach of poring over the details of the financials. Chanos discovered that the Enron partnerships were shaky at best and disastrous at worst. He shorted the stock and thereby furthered his reputation as an expert analyst.

Sensing types tend to be drawn to bottom-up investing. This is why, if we could accurately study the Enron debacle, we would undoubtedly find that most of the investors who lost their shirts were Intuitors by nature. They were buying the story and probably busily chastising their poor, ignorant Sensing brethren who simply didn't understand.

Intuitive investors are good at pattern recognition and seeing big trends. Ralph Wanger and his success at Acorn Fund come to mind. For those of you who know Ralph, he's a huge thinker in the sense that he's continually thinking about global patterns and trends and how to play them. Most of the top investors are wired this way: 60 percent of professional investors versus only 25 percent of the general population.

THINKING DECIDERS VERSUS FEELING DECIDERS: READING ANNUAL REPORTS OR READING PEOPLE

Thinkers dominate the investment world. More than 80 percent of investment professionals prefer to make decisions via thinking rather than feeling. Thinkers tend to be objective in their appraisal of a situation. They pull back from it and ask, "What are the criteria or the precedents?"

In contrast, Feelers instinctively imagine themselves in a situation and ask, "How would I feel if this were happening to me?" Thus, delivering a tough performance review is a very different experience for a Thinker than for a Feeler. The Thinker looks at the data—how the person has performed—and then delivers the feedback, typically in a candid and direct fashion. The Thinker is not asking herself, "How would I feel if I were in his shoes, hearing this review?" By contrast, the Feeler is thinking exactly that: "How would I feel if I were him?" Thinkers, therefore, tend to be seen as direct, frank, even blunt, and sometimes insensitive. Feelers tend to be more diplomatic, even evasive.

Herein lies the first tie-in with the seven behaviors. Thinkers, including most investment professionals, tend to be pretty good at practicing candor. On a continuum, they have fewer "withholds" (that is, unspoken issues that are relevant to business decisions) than do Feelers. The difference between the Thinker and the Feeler as it relates to beating the market is illustrated by their underlying beliefs:

Thinker: "I'll win by being completely objective and following a logical set of rules."

Feeler: "I'll win by factoring in the people element: reading CEOs and CFOs and determining what their real motivations and desires are."

A clear example of the Thinker's approach comes from Ted Aronson and his firm's (Aronson + Johnson + Ortiz) approach to investing. They make a point of saying that information from officials of publicly traded companies isn't reliable, so they ignore it. They don't interview senior management teams. They place virtually no credence in the Feelers' view that they can "read" leaders.

In contrast, Tom Weary of Diamond Portfolio Advisors in Los Angeles believes strongly in the human factor. His approach is very

Feeling in nature. He has devised a way of measuring the "character" of firms and thereby determining if they are bound for greatness. (Tom came up to me after I had given a speech in Los Angeles and exclaimed excitedly, "I use your approach to picking stocks!" Somewhat surprised, I responded, "I didn't know I *had* an approach." As we talked, he explained that the material in *Investment Leadership* had been useful in devising his investment strategy. You see, that's what the really smart people do: they read my books and make a lot of money!)

Here's a story that nicely captures the difference between Thinkers and Feelers:

> A Feeling brother goes on vacation and leaves his dog, Lucky, with his Thinking brother. In two days, the Feeling brother calls to inquire about the dog.
>
> Thinking Brother responds, "Oh, Lucky is dead."
>
> Feeling Brother, stunned, says, "What do you mean, dead?"
>
> "Well, he got hit by a truck and died."
>
> Feeling Brother: "Well, that's the last straw. You are just so inconsiderate, so unfeeling."
>
> Thinking Brother: "What should I have done?"
>
> "You should have said, 'Lucky has had an accident. He's not doing well.' Then when I called back the next time you could say, "I'm sorry, he's not improving." Finally, on the third call, you could say, "Lucky didn't make it, I'm so sorry." Feeling Brother, sighing heavily, says, "Well, I'm sorry I blew up at you. Anyway, how is Mom?"
>
> Thinking Brother: "She's had an accident."

This story points up the fact that Thinkers aren't trying to be rude. They are interested in telling the truth, so they do just that—sometimes too harshly, in the opinion of Feelers. Often Feelers have a very hard time breaking bad news to employees, as in the example concerning bad performance reviews or the situation of layoffs. Instead of giving it to people straight, they dance and weave and often deliver only a half-truth. When I mentioned this during a speech once, a woman sitting near the front shot up out of her chair and shouted, "That's the cruelest thing you can do!" My first thought was, "Well, thanks for revealing your preference for Thinking!" It was true: as a Thinker, this woman believed that the kindest thing to do was give it to people straight, even if it meant hurting their feelings.

Despite the overwhelming number of Thinkers in the investment arena, there are some notable exceptions. John Rogers at Ariel has a preference for Feeling, and readily admits that his Thinking president, Mellody Hobson, is better at the "tough people decisions." Another famous Feeler is Rob Arnott, who founded First Quadrant and is CEO of Research Affiliates, as well as editor-in-chief of the *Financial Analysts Journal*. When faced with the unpleasant task of laying off a number of people during a market downturn, Rob insisted on handling it personally with one-on-one interviews. Another famous Feeling investor is Jeremy Grantham. During the course of dinner one evening, I experienced him as having a warm personality and was not surprised later to find out that his MBTI showed he had a preference for Feeling over Thinking in his decisions. Another very talented investor with a preference for Feeling, as mentioned earlier in this book, is Kim Redding, CEO of K.G. Redding & Associates.

ORGANIZED (JUDGING) VERSUS FLEXIBLE (PERCEIVING): FELIX AND OSCAR (THE ODD COUPLE)

The Myers-Briggs people originally named these preferences so poorly that I have felt compelled to rename them. After all, "judging" and "perceiving" don't tell you anything! Simply put, some people like to be "planful," organized, and orderly; others prefer to go with the flow, remaining flexible and open. Much humor, like the play, movie, and television series *The Odd Couple*, is based on this common disparity. Organized people are called "judgers" in the Myers-Briggs lingo and flexible types are called "perceivers." Our experience in the investment world reveals an overwhelming majority of Judgers, the ones who are decisive and live by plans (75 percent of the investment world are Judgers, versus 60 percent in the general population). In fact, many senior investment teams have no (or at most one) Perceiver member. Notable exceptions are Perceivers such as Jeff Diermeier and Rob Arnott. (Kim Redding is the only Perceiver on his leadership team; in fact, in his entire company!) Perceivers often fit well in the role of strategist, the big-picture thinker. They like to keep their options open and enjoy hearing all the scenarios. For leadership teams that are heavy on Judgers, they must be careful not to close down conversations too quickly. Their motto could well be, "All action and no talk!," because they hate long brainstorming sessions and feel much better when a decision has been reached and they can move on it. (An old poster I once saw captures their impatience well: It shows two buzzards sitting on a tree limb, and the caption reads, "Patience, my ass, I'm gonna kill something!") Judgers must watch their tendency to pack up and move on before all the good options have been considered.

The strategies for winning, then, differ for the Judger and the Perceiver:

Judger: "I'll win in the markets by relentlessly sticking to the rules."
Perceiver: "I'll win by knowing when to change the rules."

George Soros is a good example of someone who is willing to change the rules on a moment's notice. If one of the variables in his global strategies seems to be shifting, he'll unload an entire position in an afternoon. He prides himself on flexibility. Others, such as John Rogers or Charles Brandes, pride themselves on staying the course as value investors.

Occasionally, when presented with this information, a leader will say, "Do we try to change the Judgers we have or bring in some Perceivers?" First, remember that it is possible for any type to succeed in any job. It is really a matter of desire and effort and awareness. There have been successful players in the National Basketball Association who were less than six feet tall. Not many, though, and the ones that made it had tremendous drive and heart. Typically, it is better for us average folks to do what we were designed to do: namely, work in line with our natural talents and genius. Rather than try to change a zebra's stripes to spots, it is better to get a leopard in the first place. Hiring for investment firms should be like recruiting in pro sports. If you are looking for a center on your basketball team, you will need someone with certain attributes; likewise if you need a creative strategist for your quant group.

TYPES AND CULTURES IN THE INVESTMENT WORLD

Summarizing all of the foregoing, the typical investment professional, as well as the typical team, is INTJ:

Introversion (I): Analysts and portfolio managers tend to be good at concentrating for long periods of time. They like to think and work with ideas.

Intuition (N): They tend to like complex problems and playing with theories and investment themes. They are naturally curious and often ask, "What if?"

Thinking (T): They tend to be competitive and like a good challenge. (Glenn Carlson, CEO at Brandes, when asked what he loved most about his work life, said, "I love to kick complete ass!")

Judgment (J): They are decisive and organized.

Over and over, we find that this is true of asset management teams. (*Note:* The INTJ personality profile does *not* reflect the MBTI types for sales forces, back-office staffers, or financial advisors; just the research staffs and portfolio managers.) Take a typical example, the investment leadership team at a large and successful value shop. Table 10.2 shows the breakout by preferences for the five leaders (two extroverts, three introverts, and so on).

INTJ. Given the nature of investment analysis, this is no surprise. All these traits contribute to excellent analysis and performance.

From a leadership perspective, INTJ investment firms are very strong at strategic thinking and discipline. The value shop previously mentioned, for example, has established a premier record because of its adherence to value investing principles and its discipline in sticking with its philosophy in tough times. This is very much a Rationalist investment team. From our work on investment cultures, we believe there are four basic cultures in the investment world:

1. Rationalist (heavy on intuition and thinking).
2. Guardian (heavy on sensing and judging).
3. Communalist (heavy on intuition and feeling).
4. Adventurist (heavy on sensing and perceiving).

Additional characteristics of these four cultures are listed in Table 10.3.

Using the information from all of the preceding discussion, we can now integrate personality types, cultures, and behaviors into some useful generalizations for asset management firms.

- The most common asset management personality is INTJ.
- The most common culture of asset management firms is NT or Rationalist.
- The common attributes of asset management professionals are:
  - Confidence, intelligence.
  - High expectations.
  - Direct communication style.
  - Discipline; makes and adheres to plans.
  - Detachment, objectivity.
- The values to the firm of these attributes are:
  - Decisive, creative.
  - Stretches team's talent.
  - Efficiency, clarity.
  - Sets and achieves objectives.
  - Focused on task.

TABLE 10.2   Myers-Briggs Preferences for Sample Leadership Team

Extraversion (E)		Introversion (I)	
• Focus is outside: people, places, things • Tends to "do–think–do" • Prefers verbal to written communication	**2**	• Focus is inside: ideas and feelings • Tends to "think–do–think" • Prefers written to verbal communication	**3**
Sensing (S)		Intuiting (N)	
• Linear thinking • Practical; likes details • Step-by-step approach	**1**	• Creative thinking • Theoretical; likes big picture • Jumps from idea to idea	**4**
Thinking (T)		Feeling (F)	
• Objective decision making • Tough-minded • Competitive • Goes for truth and clarity	**5**	• Subjective decision making (based on personal values) • Tender-hearted • Cooperative • Goes for warmth and kindness	**0**
Judging (J)		Perceiving (P)	
• Organized • Decisive • Planful	**5**	• Flexible • Open to new options • Goes with the flow	**0**

TABLE 10.3 Temperament and Portfolio Management

Four Temperaments	Guardian	Rationalist	Adventurer	Communalist
Animal	Beaver	Owl	Fox	Dolphin
Market View	"It's a battle to be won by patience, precision, and discipline."	"It's a challenging puzzle to be solved."	"It's a fun game to be played with flair."	"It's a garden to be weeded and cultivated for growth."
Investment Strength	Discipline and execution	Creative analysis	Fact-finding, risk seeking	Collaboration and intuition
Investment Style	Technical, rule-oriented	Value, quantification, contrarian	Growth and arbitrage	Socially conscious
Investment Roles	Traders, administrators	Analysts, strategists, economists	Researchers, brokers, hedge-fund managers	Research directors, client relationship managers
Examples	Zweig, Dreman	Buffett, Munger	Lynch	Diversity fund, Domini fund
Possible Weakness	Too rigid, clings to past, lacks flexibility	Too theoretical, lacks data	Too reckless, lacks patience	Too Idealistic, lacks toughness
Communication Style	Comparative	Conditionals	Anecdotes	Metaphors
Time Orientation	Past	Infinite	Present	Future
Needs	Membership	Competency	Freedom	Relationship
Risk Profile	Risk-averse	Risk-seeking if merited	Risk-seeking	Risk-neutral
Fears	Losing control	Being judged incompetent	Being constrained	Being rejected
Financial Propensity	To save, hoard	To take, wrest	To spend, dissipate	To give, divest

- The possible weaknesses for the firm are:
  - Arrogance, demeaning attitude.
  - Failure to appreciate.
  - Fear, gossip, CYA.
  - Unreasonable demands.
  - Aloofness, uninspirational.

Our experience of working with asset management teams is that these characteristics allow them to be very good at some of the seven behaviors (particularly candor, genius, and agreements) and weak with others.

As mentioned earlier in this chapter, Thinkers (for example, Rationalists) tend to be direct and candid. They value truth-telling and are less likely to withhold important data for fear of hurting someone's feelings. We actually find this element of working with asset managers refreshing. They are courageous in telling the truth and are mostly willing to hear it told about and to them, as well.

Rationalists also tend to be naturally gifted at finding their genius. Most investment professionals with whom we work have a deep passion for their careers. They feel genuinely grateful to be doing the work of research, analysis, portfolio management, and strategy. They don't always like their bosses or their environments, but most of them are very clear that they like the nature of the work.

Furthermore, Rationalists in the investment world (who tend to be NTs and Js as well; in other words, NTJs) are naturally gifted at the agreements portion of accountability behavior. NTJs like order and rationality and good agreements fit into that world view.

THE TOUGH BEHAVIORS FOR RATIONALISTS: CURIOSITY, RESPONSIBILITY, APPRECIATION

Just as there are three behaviors that seem to come fairly easily for Rationalists, so there are three that challenge them.

The first is curiosity. This is not to say that investment professionals aren't curious. They are, but not necessarily in the way we define it. Remember, we are talking about being open and curious in relationship to feedback. The tendency for Rationalists is to be competitive and ready for a fight. When someone challenges their thinking with a piece of feedback, they automatically go to defending their point of view. To master the first and most important behavior, Rationalists have to unlearn that instinctive behavior. They need to learn to listen better and stay open longer. They need to learn that there is an option: they can choose between debate and dialogue. The latter is an open conversation, in which the goal is to share ideas, not to win. Rationalists who can learn to do this have gained an important new tool for their kit.

Secondly, Rationalists often fail in the 100 percent responsibility portion of the accountability behavior. In part, they do this for the same reasons explained earlier. Rationalists tend to be very confident by nature. The technical term is *self-authenticating*, which is a fancy way of saying that they believe what they say is true. (More than a few Rationalists have smiled a knowing smile when I say this during presentations.) Therefore, their natural inclination when performing a postmortem is to assume that they got their portion right. Their sharp intelligence can usually defend their views as well. Thus, Rationalists really have to work at seeing a situation from a different angle; that is, playing with the question, "How might I have contributed to this poor performance?"

Years ago, I worked with an intelligent Rationalist who had studied the seven behaviors and often invoked them during meetings. When it came to this one, though, she usually invoked it—subtly—to point the finger at someone else: "The client didn't take 100 percent responsibility for following through on the assignment." Of course, another way to think of this is: What could I have done differently to encourage the client to take responsibility?

Another story like this, which leads us into the next behavior (appreciation) comes from a portfolio manager at a major Midwestern firm. I explained to him our belief that a good working relationship—or marriage—has a 5:1 ratio of praise to blame. He got excited about this fact and said, "I'm going to try that at home." The next morning I saw him and he said triumphantly, "Well, last night I said to my wife, do you know that the best marriages have a 5-to-1 ratio of praise to blame?" Then he said to her, "When was the last time you gave me some praise?" Not exactly what we had in mind as *taking* responsibility!

Finally, and not surprisingly, Rationalists have difficulty building cultures of appreciation. This is in part because of their towering ability to be critical. Analysts are paid lots of money to think critically. It's almost heretical for them to remove that thinking cap and to put on one that says, "Let's see this person with new eyes and watch him grow effortlessly in value." Say what?! Most Rationalists are a bit suspicious of the whole concept of appreciation. One portfolio manager we work with said, "If I try this stuff at home with my wife, she'll think I'm having an affair!" Their first thought usually is something along the lines of "if we constantly praise our people, they'll stop working. Or worse yet, ask for more money!"

A boss of mine once said this directly while we were traveling together. I had given the hotel maid a large tip, and he said afterward, "Don't break their rice bowl." When I asked what that meant, he responded, "If you give them too large a tip—like too much rice in their bowl—they want more next time." Though there may be some truth to this notion, our experience with firms has shown that developing a culture of appreciation has just the opposite effect. People love the environment and will actually work for less compensation because they view the culture itself as a form of payment. Firms that want to attract and retain the very best talent would be wise to experiment with appreciation as a way to gain a competitive advantage in the marketplace. As mentioned in Chapter 9 on appreciation, we recommend a 5:1 ratio of appreciation to criticism.

CHAPTER 11

Decision Rights
Establishing and Clarifying the Rules

Jim Ware

Curiosity, accountability, candor, authenticity, awareness, genius, and appreciation: Seven behaviors that high-performing investment teams adopt as their rules of engagement and that distinguish those teams from the pack. To pull all these behaviors together, we have chosen to conclude this book with something that is not as much a behavior as it is a best practice of high-performing teams: establishing and clarifying decision rights.

The best investment professionals are world-class decision makers. They take in enormous amounts of information, process it, reflect on it, and then decide—sooner rather than later, in most cases. Contrast world-class decision makers with those in the typical corporate meeting, in which information is presented, discussed, endlessly analyzed, and then . . . no, it appears that a decision is *not* forthcoming. Rather, in true "Dilbert" style, someone utters the infamous, "We'll schedule another meeting to decide."

At Focus Consulting Group, we have found that the best investment firms are committed to rapid and precise decisions. We recently facilitated an offsite session, for John Rogers and his Ariel Capital Management team, that was aimed directly at promoting efficient meetings with effective decision making. As part of the offsite, we explained our ladder of decision rights (see Figure 11.1).

The best investment firms have clearly articulated their decision rights. When the need for a decision arises, the best leaders choose how they will make the decision from a hierarchical list of options. Good leaders also specify up front who has decision rights regarding a particu-

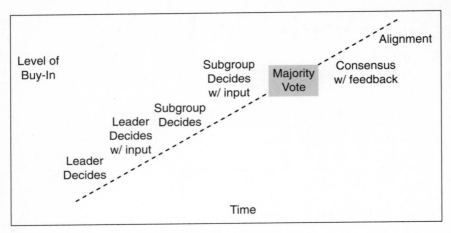

FIGURE 11.1 Decision rights.

lar matter, which speeds up the process and helps settle down the team members. Team members understand their roles in how a decision will be made. They understand whether they have a voice and a vote, or just a voice, or neither.

A LESSON FOR JOE

The following is an example of what good decision making does *not* look like.

A senior portfolio manager, Joe, assembles the team of analysts and junior portfolio managers and asks for an update on a large holding. One analyst presents the positive case for the stock. As part of the normal process, a different analyst presents the opposing, devil's-advocate, case. Discussion ensues, and finally, Joe says to his junior portfolio managers, "Well, what do you think?" At this point, the assumption in the room is that Joe is looking for consensus on this stock; he wants to talk it through until he and the three junior portfolio managers are of one mind. The discussion starts, and it soon becomes evident that all three portfolio managers do not like this stock and want it sold. After each one presents arguments, Joe scratches his head, looking concerned, and says, "Yes, I hear what you're saying, but I really want to keep it in our large-cap portfolio." The stock continues to be held. The meeting is adjourned.

As an observer of this meeting, I asked Joe what decision-making principle had guided the outcome. He responded: "Well, I tend to like consensus."

To which I replied, "You realize that wasn't consensus, right?"

Joe looked genuinely surprised. "What do you mean?" he inquired.

"That was 'leader decides with input from his team.' Consensus is very different. In consensus, you need to talk the decision through until every team member is on board, until there are no dissenting votes."

Clearly, this seemed to be new information. I pulled Joe into an empty conference room and drew the ladder chart on the whiteboard. When I had finished, I explained that decision making is always a trade-off between the amount of buy-in you are looking for and the time it takes to achieve the buy-in. I then reviewed the chart.

THE RUNGS OF THE LADDER

The simplest decisions are "leader decides." In this case, the leader needs no input and can simply tell the team what the decision is. The great benefit of this type of decision making is speed. The downside is the potential for poor buy-in. People tend to rally behind decisions that they helped make.

The next rung up the ladder is "leader decides with input." In this case, the leader solicits opinions from his or her team and then makes the decision. Joe used this choice for his team meetings. Given this choice, Joe should have explained clearly the decision rules and the role of each participant (for example, to have a voice but not a vote in the decision).

The next steps up the ladder are "subgroup decides," followed by "subgroup decides with input." These choices are similar to the first two rungs, but in this case, the leader delegates his or her authority to a subgroup. For this type of decision making, it is important for the leader initially to specify and include any constraints on the decision. If the leader challenges the subgroup's decision after the fact, his or her credibility may be damaged—after all, the leader said it was the subgroup's decision. Second-guessing the subgroup looks bad.

The next choice on the decision ladder is "majority vote." This form of decision making is the heart and soul of *Robert's Rules of Order* (all those in favor say, "Aye"; all opposed, say, "Nay"). The advantage of this form of decision making is that each person gets both a voice and a vote. The downside is that there are clear winners and losers. It is a win/lose approach.

A step up from this level is "consensus," a very sophisticated form of decision making that requires considerable skill and a collaborative mindset. When consensus is used, people are being asked to set their personal agendas aside and consider what is good for the team. Those of us schooled in typical debate-style discussions have trouble doing this. We only know how to argue for our position. Key requirements for consensus decision making are (1) enough time, and (2) a fallback plan. The latter is important because there is no guarantee that a decision will be reached using consensus.

With consensus decision making, we use a five-point scoring system. After we have talked through the issue sufficiently, we ask team members to weigh in with where they are on the following scale:

> 5 = I like the proposal and I'm totally on board.
> 4 = I like it with a minor reservation (or two).
> 3 = I like it but have a major reservation that I'd like addressed.
> 2 = I'm neutral; that is, *not* on board.
> 1 = I don't like it. I'm opposed.

The rule for true consensus is that every team member must be at level 3, 4, or 5. If anyone weighs in with a 2 or a 1 vote, consensus has not been reached and the discussion goes on. (Usually the appropriate question for the neutrals or detractors is, "What would it take to get you on board?" Then let them negotiate a win/win reformulation of the proposal.)

If, after sufficient time and negotiation, the team still cannot reach consensus, then the leader applies the fallback or backup decision-making rule. Often, this is "leader decides with input," though it could easily be "majority vote."

The final choice for decision making is alignment. This level is a special case of consensus. *Alignment* means not just that team members are on board, which could include different levels of buy-in, but that they are all enthusiastically on board. Alignment is often used for critically important decisions, such as mergers, hiring of key personnel, and new vision statements.

THE LADDER IN ACTION

When I outlined these choices for Joe, he understood, seemingly for the first time, that his preferred decision-making style for most stock-picking decisions was "leader decides with input." From that point on, his investment meetings were remarkably more efficient, and comments from team members were as follows: "It was a great relief to get that clarity, because we knew all along that we weren't going for consensus!"

Do any investment firms go for consensus in stock picking? Yes. Brandes Investment Partners uses this decision-making style in its investment meetings. As a very tight Graham and Dodd shop, it operates very effectively with thorough discussions of the analyst's idea and then a declaration by committee members of whether or not they are on board. CEO Glenn Carlson, CFA, calls this form of decision making "soft consensus," because occasionally the committee will still approve a decision over a dissenting vote. (Brandes has one of the strongest corporate cultures of any firm we've measured. This strong culture allows it to use consensus as a decision-making method, whereas a less clearly defined organization might waffle badly with this choice.)

Prior to a critical offsite planning session with his firm, Michael Sapir, CEO at ProFunds, selected "leader decides with input" as his preferred style. Michael told us, "I want to have good discussion and lots of input, but at the end of the day, the key decisions around the firm's core purpose, vision, mission, and values are mine." Team members appreciated that clarity, and the session was remarkably productive because they did not bog down in long periods of indecision. When leaders know in their minds and hearts where they stand on a certain issue, it is unproductive to spend time debating that issue. The leader makes the decision, and the team moves on.

CONCLUSION

For the reasons just stated, we have learned that when we have offsite sessions with investment firms, the smartest thing we can do up front is to describe and explain decision rights. We meet with the firm's leader and agree on what style of decision making will be used for each major decision at the session. Doing so ensures efficient and effective use of time at the offsite session.

SUMMARY

- World-class investment firms are committed to rapid and precise decision making.
- Good leaders specify up front who has decision rights on a particular matter, which speeds up the process and settles down the team members.
- Decision making always involves a tradeoff between the amount of buy-in desired and the time it takes to achieve the buy-in.

Concluding Thoughts
Measurement, Behavioral Finance, Integrity, and an Invitation for More

Jim Ware

There you have it. Seven simple steps to creating a world-beating team. Just spend a little less time on your short game, and a little more time on these behaviors, and you'll have them down in a flash. Right?

Wrong.

None of us will ever completely perfect these behaviors. Rather, adoption of these behaviors represents a lifelong commitment to continuous improvement. In fact, the language that we use to talk about them, courtesy of the Hendricks Institute, is "drift and shift." We commit to doing one of the behaviors, knowing full well that we will drift off our commitment at some point. No one will be curious all the time; no one will be impeccable around all agreements; no one will be candid in every team conversation; and so on. We stress this point because seeking perfection with regard to these behaviors will only set you up for frustration and failure. The goal is to recognize when you have drifted off your commitment and then—easefully—recommit. Just climb back on the wagon. The very best individuals and teams measure their success by the speed at which they recognize and recommit, not by a naïve and unattainable goal of perfection.

I want to stress how very different the material in this book is from the typical material read and digested by investment professionals. Most of what you deal with is intellectual in nature: you hear a case for interest rates declining or for a company's growth rate to accelerate and you agree or disagree. Either way, you take the appropriate action in your portfolio. In most cases, there is no resistance between the intellectual insight and the changed portfolio. The implementation is straightforward.

The material in this book, however, is not simply intellectual. For example, you could put this book down and think, "Yes, that makes sense. We should practice curiosity and accountability and candor, and so on." Despite this intellectual agreement—"yes, we *should* do it"—you and your team would be no closer to implementation. (The same would be true of listening to a compelling case for weight loss. You might think, "Yes, by golly, it's time for me to reduce!," but you haven't lost one ounce by having that thought.) The tough part about these behaviors is that, like weight loss, they require commitment, discipline, and follow-through.

They also require *measurement*. Just as getting on the scale periodically is a key step in successfully controlling your weight, measuring how well the behaviors are being practiced within a firm is essential in achieving and maintaining true cultural change. As Drucker said so succinctly, "what gets measured, gets done." We find this is especially true on the "soft side" of the ledger: leadership, culture, and teamwork. We have found that using measurement tools like our Culture and Values Survey and our Behavioral Scorecard allows firms to benchmark and track improvement. When these measurement tools are woven into the firm's reward system—compensation and promotion—then the culture work really gets traction!

Because so few investment teams practice these behaviors, it's easy to dismiss them in favor of the comfort of the herd. All we can say to this predictable line of reasoning is that *superior results do not come from taking the safe and easy path*. We know from working with the best investment teams that these behaviors provide a competitive advantage, but they require focused, ongoing effort. The choice, of course, is yours!

When we began this book, we fully intended to add thoughts about the integration of our work and behavioral finance. The connection is unmistakable, and we, like many, are fascinated by the findings of behavioral finance experts. We believe that these seven behaviors do act as antidotes for the common pitfalls highlighted in the literature. For example, overconfidence is a well-studied and documented misstep in reasoning; we all tend to believe that we know more than we actually do. The antidote to overconfidence lies in the first behavior, choosing curiosity over defensiveness. Overconfidence is a function of ego, and this is exactly what the curiosity behavior addresses. Be curious and open to all disconfirming evidence so that you can honestly test your theories, free of bias. Easier said than done, of course.

As this book unfolded, we realized that there was quite enough material just on the seven behaviors. Undoubtedly, our next writing endeavor will be to integrate our work with behavioral finance. In the meantime, please consider this an invitation to engage us in dialogue about this interesting topic. We have insights to share and would love to hear yours. Visit our web site, *www.focusCgroup.com*, and call or write us.

Another topic that we chose to omit was integrity. Jim Dethmer is passionate about it and would have written the chapter for us. He is fond of asking investment leaders, "How do you define *integrity?*" Their response usually boils down to a version of *do the right thing*. Beyond that, we rarely get much practical direction. Jim, however, has thought extensively about the practical side of integrity and has operationalized it on three levels: legal, ethical, and energetic. (Remember, all our work boils down to a simple test: Does a behavior increase or decrease your energy? Integrity follows this same law. When we live and act with integrity, it increases our available energy.) This is fascinating stuff, and vitally important to the investment world, given all the misbehavior and the new compliance environment. Therefore, we decided integrity was worthy of an entire book, not merely a chapter in this one. The preceding invitation, concerning ongoing dialogue, applies to integrity as well. Please contact us. We'd be happy to share our thoughts.

All that said, we hope to hear from you. In the meantime, here's wishing you the best of success in your professional and personal endeavors.

ACHIEVING A PERFORMANCE CULTURE: RESOURCES FROM FOCUS CONSULTING GROUP

In our work with top investment firms around the world, we have identified best practices and developed methodologies that help teams achieve and maintain performance cultures. These successful teams share the following characteristics:

- Ability to attract and retain top investment talent.
- The right people in the right positions, thereby promoting high levels of employee engagement and commitment.
- World-class decision making.
- Smooth conflict resolution process.
- Elimination of drama and negativity on the team.
- A clear, compelling vision that is understood and supported across the organization.
- Well-defined values and adherence to a well-defined code of behavior to support those values.
- Clearly defined leadership development and succession planning.
- Systematic measurement of culture, leadership, and team performance to monitor improvements.

Our approach to cultural change gains immediate traction because it creates an environment of shared accountability. With the ongoing support of the senior leadership team and the direct involvement—and ownership—of each team member, cultural change is accelerated.

Our techniques include an integrated program of individual and team assessments, offsite team workshops, executive coaching, comprehensive communications, hiring for fit, and ongoing measurement, to ensure that a performance culture is both achieved and maintained over the long term.

For more information about how Focus Consulting Group can help your organization achieve a performance culture, please visit us at www.focusCgroup.com, or e-mail us at jware@focusCgroup.com.

Afterword

This team of experienced and respected investment consultants has provided a unique window into the best practices of successful investment teams. Candor, accountability, awareness, curiosity, authenticity, genius, and appreciation: these practices are the grist and grit of top leaders and other members of high-impact investment organizations.

These practices support personal growth. Equally importantly, they are the antidote for corporate sludge: the byproduct of poor communication, dishonesty, and fear; the behaviors that slow organizations to a crawl. In the investment arena, perhaps more so than any other, speed and efficiency are paramount and sludge can be fatal. In our business consulting and coaching, we too have discovered that applying concepts and strategies from the field of personal growth to the hard-charging, results-oriented world of investment and business can produce tremendous results and create sustained energy for rapid growth, especially in times of change and challenge.

Additionally, as a physician and medical scientist, Eddie often sees change and leadership through the biological lens. Research shows that there is a biochemical link between these behaviors and the nervous system, and thus the entire body. Practicing candor, accountability, awareness, curiosity, authenticity, and appreciation leads to clear physiological benefits, such as stress reduction and clarity of thought, which, in turn, nurture creativity and productivity.

We have seen time and again that without commitment to these practices, growth is not sustainable, stress is inevitable, and success is unpredictable. In contrast, when one embraces these behaviors, radical change becomes possible—and the payoffs are extraordinary.

Our thanks to these authors for further charting the course and lending their experience and passion to the growing body of evidence initially assembled by Gay and Kathlyn Hendricks. The investment world is in good hands.

With warm respect,

Kate Ludeman, PhD
Eddie Erlandson, MD
Authors of *Radical Change, Radical Results*

Endnotes

PREFACE

1. Scott Thurm, "Teamwork Raises Everyone's Game," *Wall Street Journal*, November 7, 2005, B8.)

INTRODUCTION

1. James C. Collins and Jerry I. Porras, *Built to Last* (New York: HarperBusiness, 1994); Jim Collins, *Good to Great* (New York: HarperCollins, 2001).
2. Jerry Useem, "Jim Collins on Tough Call," *Fortune*, June 27, 2005, 94.
3. Kate Ludeman and Eddie Erlandson, *Radical Change, Radical Results* (Chicago: Dearborn Trade, 2003).
4. Cited in Viv Groskop, *Business Life*, October 2005, 28.
5. Jack Welch, *Winning* (San Francisco: HarperCollins, 2005), 156.
6. Bill Williams, *Trading Chaos, Applying Expert Techniques to Maximize Profits* (Hoboken, N.J.: John Wiley & Sons, 1995), 96.
7. Jim Rudd, telephone interview, August 2005.
8. *www.humansyn.com*
9. Robert J. Kriegel and Louis Patler, *If It Ain't Broke, Break It! and Other Unconventional Wisdom for a Changing Business World* (New York: Warner Books, 1991). This study was based on research with 80,000 managers.
10. *Id.* at 214.

CHAPTER 1

1. Hoboken, N.J.: John Wiley & Sons, 2004.
2. Gary Brinson, "Organizational Culture," in *Managing Investment Firms: People and Culture* [conference proceedings] (AIMR, 1996).
3. Capital Resource Advisors, July 21, 2002; available at *www.cradv.com*. Last accessed 29 June 2003.

4. Jim Collins and Jerry Porras, *Built to Last* (New York: Harper Business, 1994).
5. Jim Ware, *Investment Leadership: Building a Winning Culture for Long-Term Success* (Hoboken, N.J.: John Wiley & Sons, 2004), 149.
6. Daniel Goleman, *Emotional Intelligence* (New York: Bantam, 1995).
7. David Fisher, personal interview with author, Los Angeles, CA, 2005.

CHAPTER 2

1. Chris Argyris, "Teaching Smart People How to Learn," *Harvard Business Review,* May-June 1991, 99–109.
2. Edward DeBono, *Six Thinking Hats* (San Francisco: HarperCollins, 1991).

CHAPTER 3

1. Dennis Byrne, "Why Do We Always Assign Blame?" *Chicago Tribune*, September 5, 2005, 23.
2. Steve Chapman, "Disaster Leads to Premature Blame Game," *Chicago Tribune*, September 4, 2005, Section 2, 9.
3. The time-honored abbreviation for "cover your ass."
4. Jim Collins, *Good to Great* (New York: HarperCollins, 2001), 78.

CHAPTER 4

1. David Allen, *Getting Things Done* (New York: Penguin, 2001).
2. Cited in Gay Hendricks and Kate Ludeman, *The Corporate Mystic* (New York: Bantam Trade Books, 1996), 124.

CHAPTER 5

1. *The Oxford Desk Dictionary* (New York: Berkeley Books, 1997), 104.
2. Quoted in a speech by Michael Mauboussin, San Diego, California, January 2005.

CHAPTER 6

1. Kate Ludeman and Eddie Erlandson, *Radical Change, Radical Results* (Chicago: Dearborn Trade, 2003), 109.
2. *Id.* at 143.
3. John Lee, *The Missing Peace in Recovery* (unpublished manuscript, 2005).
4. Personal interview, August 19, 2005.
5. Merrillyn Kosier, executive vice president, Ariel Capital Management, telephone interview with authors, August 2005.
6. *Id.*

CHAPTER 7

1. Jane Spencer, "Applications from Behavioral Finance," *Wall Street Journal*, July 21, 2005, D1.
2. An organization called HeartMath (*www.heartmath.com*) has evidence to show that the heart is more than a muscle; it actually contains practical wisdom, like our brains.
3. Malcolm Gladwell, *Blink* (New York: Little, Brown, 2005).
4. *www.ccl.org*; last accessed 12 November 2005.
5. Daniel Goleman, *Emotional Intelligence* (New York: Bantam, 1995); Daniel Goleman, Richard Boyatzis, and Annie McKee, *Primal Leadership* (Boston: Harvard Business School Press, 2002).
6. Goleman, Boyatzis, and McKee, *Primal Leadership*, 206.
7. Jane Marcus and Terry Bacon, *Developing Better Asset Management Leadership* (Heidrick & Struggles, 2004).
8. Goleman, Boyatzis, and McKee, *Primal Leadership*, 102.
9. Marcus and Bacon, *Developing Better Asset Management Leadership*, 4.
10. Edward M. Hallowell, *Connect* (New York: Random House, 1999), 103.
11. *http://www.alberteinstein.info/*; last accessed 11 November 2005.
12. Robert Koppel, *The Intuitive Trader* (Hoboken, N.J.: John Wiley & Sons, 1996).
13. Bill Williams, *Trading Chaos: Applying Expert Techniques to Maximize Profits* (Hoboken, N.J.: John Wiley & Sons, 1995), 156.
14. Richard McCall, *The Way of the Warrior-Trader: The Financial Risk-Taker's Guide to Samurai Courage, Confidence, and Discipline* (New York: Irwin Professional Publishing, 1996), 132.

15. Edward Toppel, *Zen in the Markets* (New York: Warner, 1994), 54.
16. Quoted in Koppel, *The Intuitive Trader,* 143.
17. For a complete description, see James Ware, *The Psychology of Money: An Investment Manager's Guide to Beating the Market* (New York: John Wiley & Sons, 2000).
18. *www.berkshirehathaway.com*; last accessed 12 November 2005.
19. Sandra Weintraub, *The Hidden Intelligence* (Burlington, MA, Butterworth Heineman, 1998), 152.
20. Cited in Weintraub, *The Hidden Intelligence,* 152.
21. Peter Senge, *The Fifth Discipline* (New York: Doubleday, 1990), 312.
22. Gladwell, *Blink,* 215.
23. One resource we recommend in this regard is the book, *Embracing Your Inner Critic: Turning Self-Criticism into a Creative Asset,* by Hal and Sidra Stone (San Francisco: Harper, 1993).

CHAPTER 8

1. *www.berkshirehathaway.com*; last accessed 2 November 2005.
2. WorldatWork staff, "Majority of Managers Unprepared to Lead Future Workforce," September 19, 2005. Available at http://resourcepro.worldat-work.org/livelink/livelink/Majority_of_Managers_Unprepared_to_Lead_Future_Workforce.html?func=doc.Fetch&nodeId=831098&docTitle=Majority+of+Managers+Unprepared+to+Lead+Future+Workforce&vernum=1; last accessed 18 November 2005.

CHAPTER 9

1. Quoted in Malcolm Gladwell, *Blink* (New York: Little, Brown, 2005), 38.

CHAPTER 10

1. James Ware, *The Psychology of Money: An Investment Manager's Guide to Beating the Market* (New York: John Wiley & Sons, 2000).
2. Jim Ware, *Investment Leadership: Building a Winning Culture for Long-Term Success* (Hoboken, N.J.: John Wiley & Sons, 2004).

Index